Financial Freedom

Retire Now With Dividend Stocks

The Sick Economist

Other Works by The Sick Economist
(Books available on Amazon.com)

Your First Biotech Million: How to Earn Your Fortune in Biotech Stocks

Money Mind: *Psychological Strategies To Dominate Stock Market Investing*

SickEconomics.com - A blog about healthcare investing.

Acknowledgements

Special thanks to the Notorious Professor S, Ryan M, and my always supportive family.

"I work like a slave to become a master."
-Big Daddy Kane

Disclaimer

No content published in this book constitutes a recommendation that any particular security, portfolio of securities, transaction or investment strategy is suitable for any specific person. You further understand that neither the author nor their affiliates are advising you personally concerning the nature, potential, value or suitability of any particular security, portfolio of securities, transaction, investment strategy or other matter. To the extent that any of the content published in this book may be deemed to be investment advice or recommendations in connection with a particular security, such information is impersonal and not tailored to the investment needs of any specific person. You understand that an investment in any security is subject to a number of risks, and that discussions of any security published in this book will not contain a list or description of relevant risk factors.

This book is not intended to provide tax, legal, insurance or investment advice, and nothing in the book should be construed as an offer to sell, a solicitation of an offer to buy, or a recommendation for any security by *The Sick Economist* or any third party. You alone are solely responsible for determining whether any investment, security or strategy, or any other product or service, is appropriate or suitable for you based on your investment objectives and personal and financial situation. You should consult an attorney or tax professional regarding your specific legal or tax situation.

Contents

Introduction: Jailbreak! 1
Part 1: Essential Concepts and Core Holdings 10
    Chapter 1: The Good Old Days 11
    Chapter 2: Common Advice; Commonly Wrong 23
    Chapter 3: Fallen Angels 32
    Chapter 4: Dividend Growth Investing 44
    Chapter 5: European Stocks 50
    Chapter 6: Big Pharma, Big Dividends 59
    Chapter 7: Energy Stocks - Powering Your Retirement 65
Part 2: Special Vehicles 74
    Chapter 8: REITs - Trustworthy Dividends 75
    Chapter 9: Mortgage REITs - Solid Paper 85
    Chapter 10: BDCs - Small Loans, Big Dividends 92
    Chapter 11: Preferred Stocks - For Those Who Prefer Safe Income 99
    Chapter 12: Closed End Funds - Open the Door to Income 106
    Chapter 13: Borrow Your Income 120
Part 3: The Real World 128
    Chapter 14: Sample Portfolio - The Kid 129
    Chapter 15: Model Portfolio - The Professional 147
    Chapter 16: Model Portfolio - The Pre-Retiree 164
    Chapter 17: Model Portfolio - The Retiree "Forever Young" 182
    Chapter 18: The Knowledge Dividend 193

Introduction: Jailbreak!

Have you ever noticed how many popular films and books tell the story of a man who escapes from jail? Typically, the hero of the story has been imprisoned for a crime he did not commit. When the hero relies on perseverance and intellect to escape his confinement, the audience cheers. If you simply Google "Escape from jail movie," hundreds of entries pop up. One of the more prominent listings is an article entitled, "19 Best Prison Escape Movies of All Time" by Screenrant Magazine.

19? I could see one or two great flicks, but the 19 Greatest of All Time?

In fact, the obsession with men (and it is mostly men) who escape from jail is not even just an American obsession. Hundreds of years ago, one of the hottest selling novels in Europe was The Count of Monte Cristo, the tale of a good man who is wrongly sent to the gulag and, you guessed it, busts out of that place and proceeds to mete out righteous justice to the men who framed him. These tales permeate most cultures and times. Some might even say that the Exodus of the Israelites from Ancient Egypt, as transmitted to billions of Jews, Muslims, and Christians through the holy texts, is in fact the greatest jailbreak of all time! Of course, the Israelites weren't technically in jail, but rather enslaved, which is sort of like being in jail forever through no fault of their own.

Why are tales of imprisonment and self-actualized freedom so appealing across most cultures and epochs?

Could it be that an enormous number of people see themselves as serving a sentence for a crime they didn't commit? Could it be that many, many people live lives of quiet desperation, where they very much feel in bondage, even if no physical chains or bars hold them back? Could it be that, even though we pray for divine help to release us from our servitude, who we really wish would help us…is us?

If you are reading this book, it's very unlikely that you are reading it from an actual jail cell. It's also very unlikely that you are literally kept as a slave (although, even now, some people still endure physical bondage).

But something still ain't right. Society learned a long time ago how to control us, dominate us, and exploit us without a single whip or chain. Money may or may not be the root of all evil, but it certainly does make a lot of people do things that they don't want to do. Every day, millions upon millions of people across this Earth squander their precious time doing things they really don't want to do, because they need the money.

I wrote this book to help you increase the freedom in your life. I wrote this book to help you stand up to organizations or people in your life who have been exploiting and abusing you. I wrote this book to help you take your life back, whether you are 25, 55, or 75.

The way that you take your life back in the modern world is to make sure that money is working for you, rather than you working for it. As Sir Francis Bacon is famous for saying, "Money is an excellent servant, but a cruel master." I am going to teach you how to create passive income through dividend stock investing. It won't be quick, and it won't be easy, but I wrote this book to help you make a plan to become the master of your own life.

I know I can teach you how to do it. Because I broke out myself. If I can go from financial servitude to mastery of my money and my life, then you can, too.

My Story

I will admit right off the bat that I am a lucky guy. I was born to a well-to-do, if not rich, family that provided an outstanding education for me, and allowed me to graduate from a prestigious college debt free. I even got an inheritance in the low six figures, bestowed upon me over a series of years. But sometimes, when you are high born, that just means you have farther to fall.

I had inherited enough money to do something, but not enough to do nothing, so I did what most kids in my position did after college; I got a job. It was horrible. In exchange for what was considered high pay for a new college graduate, the owner of the company had figured out a way for him to get rich by setting up a white-collar sweatshop. Me and my fellow graduates worked seventy to eighty hours a week month after month, year after year. We got 10% of the value we produced while the owner of the company got 90%. That didn't seem fair to me, so I quit. Got another job. Guess what? Same thing.

It soon became clear to my young self that I was never going to make the kind of money that I dreamed of, or live a lifestyle I thought was fair, working for someone else. So, I started a business. And failed. And lost a lot of money. Chastened, and scared, I went back to having a job. Once again, it just gave me a nauseating feeling to watch someone else reap most of the benefit of my long hours and hard work. So, I tried to start another business. I failed again. And lost a lot of money again. This pattern repeated itself often throughout my 20s. I was substantially poorer at 29 then I had been at 21. I frequently woke up at night in a cold sweat, overwhelmed by feelings of frustration, desperation, and shame.

By age 30, I had settled into a "good" career in medical sales. I was lucky by most measures. I made good money. I didn't have a boss directly on top of me. I got to spend time around refined people. But it still felt wrong. No matter how much I sold, the company only wanted to know how much more I was going to sell the next month. I won various awards and honors, but within weeks of winning my little gold star, my boss only wanted to know how much more I was going to bring in. I would routinely see older sales people laid off; decades of faithful service to the company would be rewarded by one month of severance pay and over-priced COBRA health insurance. Even when times were good, it all just felt wrong to me. After losing so much money in my various failed entrepreneurial ventures, I needed a job, but I hated having a job. My existence as a mouse in a corporate maze made me sick every day.

So, I did the only thing that I thought that I could do. I saved. And saved. And saved. I drove used cars. I lived in neighborhoods that were so "up and coming" that I couldn't let people visit me after sundown. I shopped at Marshalls.

This frugal lifestyle was very expensive in other ways. I once broke up with a girl when she started crying after she saw the "new" used car I had procured. One girl dumped me when a homeless man defecated on the sidewalk outside my building with us just a few feet away. Apparently, she didn't like the neighborhood I was living in, and had fears about the kind of future that I would be able to provide for her. I had a marriage that lasted less than a year when it became clear that I had foolishly wed a woman who just didn't understand my burning desire to break away from Corporate America. I can look back at all of these incidents now and laugh. But it was far from funny at the time, and I limped through my early 30s in an anxious and depressed state.

As time went by, it became clear that I was much better at owning businesses than starting or running them. What I mean about that is that my stock market investments started to win. There were frightening times like the great financial crisis of '09, but somehow I just kept going. When everyone else was selling, some little voice inside me said, "keep going," and I would put almost all of my hard won sales commissions into stocks. I don't know if I was any smarter than anyone else; I was probably just more desperate. Every day in my corporate job, my invisible chains felt heavier and heavier; after failing so many times as an entrepreneur, the accumulation of stock market wealth seemed like the only remaining route of escape.

One day I turned around, and I had been saving and investing for twenty years. Much like that prisoner breaking rocks in the sun, the weeks had turned into months, and the months had turned into years, and I was still taking orders from corporate bosses who regularly demonstrated that my happiness meant nothing to them. But my assets were growing. On some level, I knew that I was approaching a financial space where I might not need that corporate paycheck anymore. But, how? I knew lots of rich people from my privileged upbringing. It was quite obvious that most of them did nothing every day. It was also quite obvious that it was purely a financial equation that allowed them to live a life of leisure. But how, exactly, did they do it?

The question became more and more pressing as time went on. In the aftermath of the 2009 financial crisis, the Federal Reserve, the government agency in charge of regulating our currency and our interest rates, had lowered rates to historically unprecedented levels, and then just left them there. Despite endless debates and the hand wringing of pundits and financial analysts, as I write this book today, interest rates are the lowest they have been in a thousand years or more. What I had always learned was that stocks were for accumulating wealth, and bonds were for retirees who wanted to reap safe income from that wealth. Now the Fed had broken the equation by taking away those safe interest payments.

That means that in order for me to quit working for a corporate paycheck and start living off my assets, I would have to start selling stock. That idea certainly felt bad! I had toiled for more than twenty years to fill up my "money bucket" and now suddenly, at only age 43, I was supposed to slowly but surely empty my "money bucket" over the rest of my potentially long life? The thought gave me a feeling of dread that slithered out of my guts and wrapped around my mind like a boa constrictor. I didn't want to keep running on my gerbil wheel, but I didn't want to start selling the stocks that I had so lovingly collected over the years. I needed to find a way to generate income from my investments, without endangering my wealth too much.

Earning money for a company that didn't care about me gave me a terrible feeling, and the only action that seemed to make that feeling go away was to study personal finance. I knew that all of those rich friends of mine still did just about nothing every day, even with interest rates at 1%. If they could do it, there had to be a way for me to do it. So I studied, and I studied. For the first few years of my 40s, in fact, you could say that I really had two jobs. During the day I worked in medical offices, hospitals, and clinics selling products for whatever commission I could wrangle, and at night I learned all about stock dividends. What exactly were dividends? Where did they come from? Why did a company pay them (or not pay them?) What could go wrong? And was it really true that most companies only paid 2 or 3% dividends?

It was my investigation around this last question, and my resulting mastery of the topic, that finally set me free. After a lot of investigation, a lot of learning, and a lot of scary trial and error, I found more and more investments that could pay me quarterly or monthly dividends of 5%, 7%, 9%, or even 11%. Instead of waking up every morning and dreading a job that I didn't want to do, I started to look forward to mornings, because mornings were the time when my dividends appeared in my brokerage account. It started out small, as if the tooth fairy had visited and left me a $20 bill when I was sleeping. But as my knowledge of dividend investing grew, and my confidence in my knowledge grew, so did my dividend income. Instead of waking up to find $20 in my bank account, it became $40. Then $140. Then $400. Then…..you get the idea.

Of course, one of the most famous jailbreak scenes of all time is from The Shawshank Redemption. After years of laborious and risky work, our hero, Andy Dufresne, crawls through the hole he has chiseled in the jail wall, through a sewer pipe, and emerges to dramatic freedom outside of the jail. We savor the drama as Andy is drenched in cleansing rain. For the first time in years, Andy feels like a free man.

After all of the anxiety and disgust that my corporate career caused, you would think that I would have had a dramatic Andy Dufresne moment when I realized that I didn't need a paycheck from my bosses anymore. You would think that the day that the dividend fairy left me enough to pay my bills outright I would have seen the heavens open up and heard the singing of angels. But I didn't.

It's hard to know why. Perhaps because my impending financial freedom wasn't a surprise. It just slowly happened, bit by bit. Just like the way Andy Dufresne slowly chipped away at the tunnel in his jail cell. When I finally crawled out of my hole, I had a feeling of disbelief, as if I were watching a movie called The Corporate Redemption, with me as the star. But I knew how the movie would end. I had done the math thousands of times.

Who I Can Help

I only tell this story about me to give you an idea, an inspiration, about what is very possible for you. Maybe your story is somewhat different. Maybe you actually do have your own business, but it's not what you hoped, and you need to find a way out. Maybe you're in a bad family business and you need to establish some independence. Maybe your corporate career has been good enough, but, as you age, you know that it's time to look to a new, more independent time in your life. You can use the very same techniques that I did to amass dividend stocks that will create passive income for you.

I took a lot of financial beatings over the years so that you don't have to. In the chapters that follow, I will help you understand each kind of dividend-paying security, and how the security may fit into your overall financial plan. Towards the end of this book, we will examine some specific life scenarios and apply what we have learned to create model portfolios that will increase financial freedom in each of the following scenarios.

-If you are just starting out in life, but you already have a creeping feeling that Corporate America is not for you, I can help.

-If you are already middle aged, have some funds saved, but only have a vague notion of how those funds can benefit you, I can help.

-If you are approaching the end of your career, or have been told that your career is over whether or not you want it to be, I can help.

-If you are already retired, and wondering how on earth you are supposed to generate income when bonds only pay 2%, I can help.

Who I CANNOT help are readers who just want specific stock tips handed to them. There are plenty of investor services that will do that for you, and plenty of financial advisors who will be happy to pick specific stocks for you. That's a fine route to take, but it's not the route I offer in the pages that lie ahead.

This book is more of a training manual to help you fend for yourself. As the saying goes, "Hand a man a fish and you feed him for a day; teach him to fish and you feed him for a lifetime."

My goal is to turn you into an outstanding fisherman of passive income. I want this book to be your first step on your journey to waking up in the morning and finding "magic money" in your bank account. Except for you, it won't be magic. It will be something that you made happen because you had a burning desire to be free.

Let's get down to business.

Part 1: Essential Concepts and Core Holdings

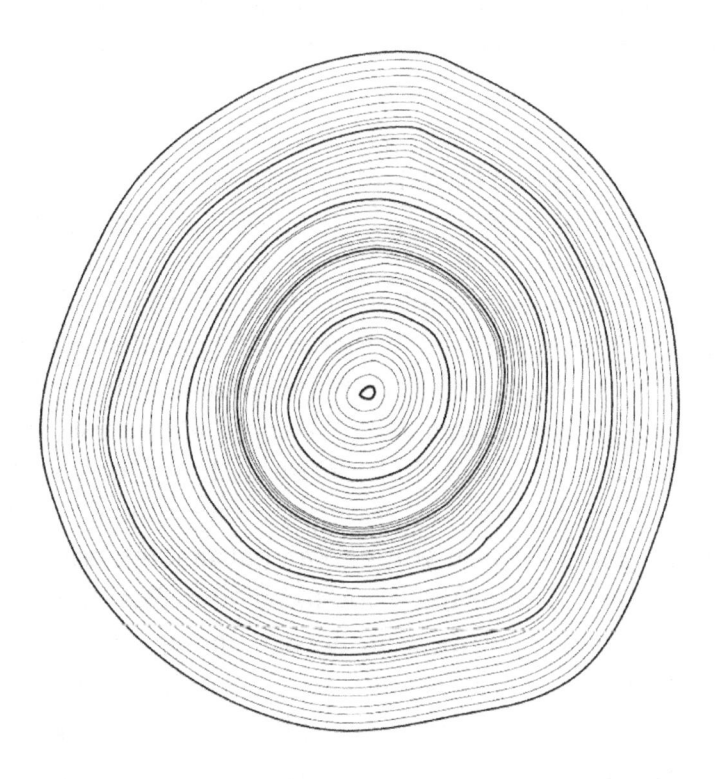

Chapter 1: The Good Old Days

Are you familiar with the term "The Greatest Generation?" This term refers to the wave of Americans born roughly between 1900 and 1930. This demographic of Americans earned this moniker by surviving the Great Depression, grinding to victory in World War II, and fending off nuclear disaster while halting the global advance of Communism. Great indeed!

But what a lot of people don't realize is that the Greatest Generation also enjoyed the greatest retirement of all time. They lucked into the greatest scenario for retirement the world had ever known. If you were born in 1920, then you were 65 in 1985. Financial conditions in 1985 were the exact OPPOSITE of today. Any moron could retire with ease, and millions upon millions of morons did.

What was the special sauce that made retirement so easy for that generation of Americans? Simple. Sky high interest rates. Just as today's interest rates are uncommonly low, from 1980 to the turn of the century, American interest rates were historically high, even though inflation was low. The result was that an unprecedented number of modest, middle class individuals could stop working at 55 or 60 and live off passive income from very secure bonds until 75, 80, or even longer.

When I say "secure" I mean rock-solid secure. The typical conservative retiree would have an assortment of CDs (certificate of deposits), treasury notes, and municipal bonds. All of these were insured by the government in one way or another, and as of 1985, any old grandma could earn 6, 7 or even 8% guaranteed interest for decades to come. If grandma got a little more daring and bought corporate bonds, even bonds of well-known, blue-chip corporations, she could reap 9 or 10%!

Today, the same grandma would be lucky to earn 0.9% interest on the same bonds. Same grandma, same fixed income securities, literally 1/10 of the income that she would have collected 35 years ago. No wonder people today feel screwed! Just to give you an idea of the magnitude of the generational difference in interest rates and what it means in a practical sense, check out this chart:

Expected Cash flow from $1,000,000

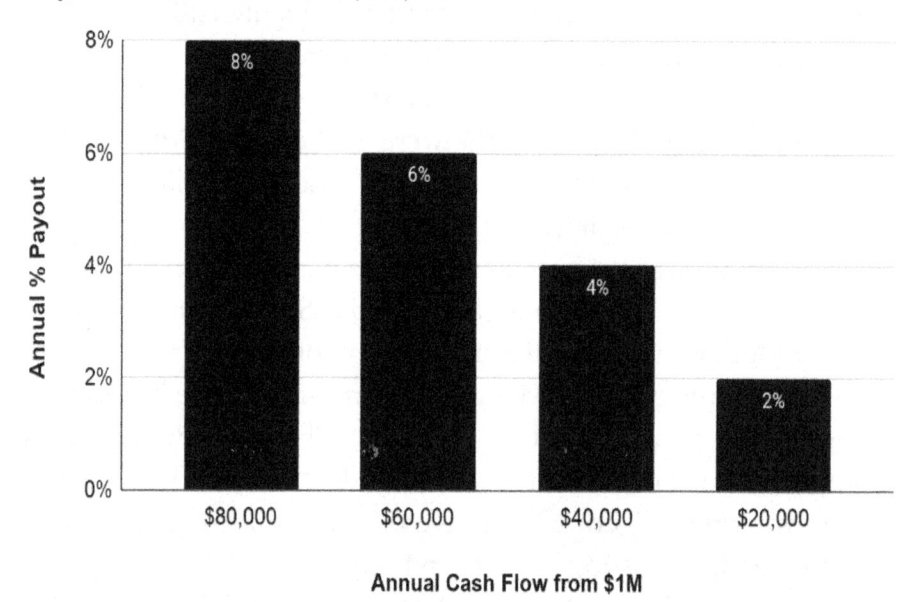

Annual Cash Flow from $1M	Annual % Payout
$80,000	8%
$60,000	6%
$40,000	4%
$20,000	2%

Figure 1

As you can see, the percentage of passive income that you can earn on your investments can make a dramatic difference to your lifestyle. The Greatest Generation had the greatest luck of all time when it came to options for passive income. Today's investors face a transformed landscape.

What Happened?

In life, all kinds of things happen for no reason at all, but in economics, everything happens for a reason. This book is mostly about solutions for today's passive income investor, but before we get to solutions, it's good to understand the problem, and how that problem came to be.

America went through a rough patch in the 1970s. A very rough patch. Inflation soared out of control, almost reaching levels that are commonly associated with developing markets. It got particularly bad in the late 70s and early 80s, when annual inflation hit 12%.

There are a lot of reasons why inflation flew out of control this way. An arab oil embargo against the United States had shocked energy prices. Strong labor unions had the power to constantly ask for higher wages. Some think that the advent of big government social programs like Medicare helped unchain the inflation beast.

Suffice it to say, when President Reagan was elected in 1980, he made it his solemn mission to win the war against runaway inflation. The chief general that he chose to wage this war was Paul Volcker, who became head of the Federal Reserve.

Volcker was quite a character and 100% committed to doing whatever was necessary. If you like history at all, I would recommend looking up images of Paul Volker on the internet. You'll immediately realize that the world of 1982 was a different galaxy because you'll see Volcker chomping on one of his trademark cigars in the middle of an indoor congressional meeting. Volcker meant to rein in inflation, and he wasn't messing around.

So the new Fed chair applied radical shock therapy. He raised interest rates even higher than the rate of inflation. Volcker hit rates so hard that the ten-year treasury note, a bellwether for these kinds of measurements, actually hit 15.68% in 1981! This means that you could lend Uncle Sam $100,000 in 1981 and he would owe you payments of $15,680 each and every year for the next decade, guaranteed by the full faith and credit of the American Federal Government. How is that for passive income?

Of course, it didn't all feel like such a great deal in 1981. Receiving interest payments of 15% isn't so great when annual inflation is running at 12%. But that is where the luck came in.

Volcker's radical shock therapy worked. The aggressive approach caused two sharp recessions, a lot of controversy, and a lot of gnashing of teeth, but Reagan and Volcker held fast. By 1986, annual inflation in America had fallen to a mere 1.9%.

You know what didn't fall? The interest rates that the federal and municipal (local) governments were obligated to pay when they issued bonds in 1981 for ten or thirty years. An entire generation of lucky geezers purchased guaranteed government bonds at 10% or more, while inflation fell to just 1.9%. These payments were locked in for decades. No wonder one of the most popular shows of the 1980s was "The Golden Girls."

One of the laws of physics is that objects in motion tend to stay in motion. The laws of economics are similar. Even with inflation dead, interest rates stayed high for almost two decades. They slowly drifted down and down, but as late as 2000, you could still get 6.58% on a ten-year treasury note. Compare that to less than 2% today. The environment of high interest rates from 1980 to the early 2000s lead to certain pieces of financial advice becoming canonized as financial gospel.

The first piece of financial advice that became gospel is that bonds are almost always safe, and thus a core product for most conservative passive income investors. As Warren Buffett used to say, "stocks are a great way to get rich; bonds are a great way to stay rich." There are a few reasons why this advice became the norm.

With interest rates so high, you could easily achieve durable passive income through the purchase of bonds guaranteed by the government. Treasury notes are guaranteed by the full faith and credit of the Federal Government. Certificates of Deposit, which in that era paid ample interest, were guaranteed by the FDIC, a federal agency. Municipal bonds were tax free, and guaranteed by state and local governments. Even corporate bonds had legal restrictions called "covenants." Covenants were financial guidelines that borrowing companies were legally bound to follow that acted as protections to investors. Covenants were like guard rails on a road. Even though corporate bonds were not guaranteed by the government, these covenants would make it harder to drive a corporate car off the cliff without investors getting plenty of warning. Today, most corporate bonds have been stripped of covenants. If management drives the corporate car off the road, that's just too bad for investors.

The second piece of conventional wisdom that became ingrained in financial advice was not only that bonds were safe, but you could still make good money on the bonds themselves. In other words, not only would the interest payments be lucrative for an investor, but the price of the bond itself would probably go up on the open market. Why would that be?

Well, think about those 15% notes from 1981, and think about the same ten-year treasury notes earning just 6.8% in 2000. If you had bought notes at 12 or 13%, and a few years later the only new notes available on the market paid 7%, then your older treasury notes would be worth more. A lot more. Year after year, decade after decade, interest rates slowly went down, meaning that legions of "golden girl" retirees actually made a killing on the mega high interest bonds they had purchased in the 1980s and 90s.

If bond income was always safe, and the market price of the bonds typically appreciated as well, that meant that everyone should own bonds. Everyone. I personally know many older, ultra-conservative investors who retired for decades only on bonds. But the standard advice that most financial planners would have given would have been for a youngish retiree to own the "60/40" portfolio. In other words, 60% stocks for growth, 40% bonds for income and security. The idea was that bonds would often go up when stocks went down. In fact, this advice worked great for decades. According to portfoliocharts.com, the "classic" 60/40 portfolio returned in excess of 8% for many years throughout the 80s and 90s. This means that, even with a large portion of your assets being in guaranteed bonds, you would have doubled your money every nine years.

You may have heard the term "black swan event." While it's not a common term in everyday language, it's a critical term in economics. Remember when I said that in economics, much like physics, objects in motion tend to stay in motion? The black swan event is the occurrence that causes that motion to come to a screeching halt. The Black Swan is an unexpected event that crashes the system and changes everything. In the world of geopolitics, the 9/11 attacks were a black swan. In the world of economics, the first major black swan of the 21st century was the great financial crisis of 2008/09.

The causes and results of the financial crisis, which started with mortgages and spread to everything, everywhere, run deep enough to merit a book all in themselves. Suffice it to say, things got bad, fast. Instead of inflation, which had been the bete noire of the Reagan generation, for the first time in modern history, America was confronted with deflation. The crisis crushed our economy so badly that people and organizations were not spending at all. They were nursing huge losses and hoarding any money they could get their hands on. The result could have actually been falling prices, the opposite of inflation. This phenomenon had occurred in Japan at the end of the 20th century, and did tremendous damage to the Japanese lifestyle for decades. Economists knew that deflation, once it takes root, is very hard to exorcise.

So America had a new boogeyman. Deflation. And in order to banish deflation, the Federal Reserve radically lowered interest rates. Interest rates dropped like a rock from 5.25% to effectively 0% in less than a year. It was shock therapy again, except just the opposite of what Volcker had done. The Fed really, really wanted individuals and organizations to borrow money, and spend money, and they were willing to go to almost any lengths to keep the Titanic from sinking. Many critics of the radical new policy felt that such low interest rates were unnatural, and worried about collateral damage. The Fed luminaries replied that the micro rates were just temporary, and more normal rates would quickly be restored when the ship righted itself.

That was twelve years ago. In 2008, the ten-year treasury note (a bellwether interest rate that the Fed only controls indirectly) hit an all time low of 2.16%. Between then and now, it slowly crawled back to a high of 3.05%, only to plummet again to 0.64% during the worst of the coronavirus crisis. At the dawn of the 21st century, that same rate was 6.39% (Data from macrotrends.net).

That Newtonian law of physics had made its weight felt in the world of economics. Micro interest rates that were supposed to be temporary just kept going.

Looking Forward

No one has a crystal ball, but it seems very likely to me that interest rates will remain very low for many years to come. A lot of experts agree with me. One reason is simple momentum; society has reorganized itself around ultra low interest rates, and business people are used to paying 2 or 3% on a loan. Without a black swan event, nothing changes. But there are two more fundamental reasons why I would guess that we will be living with micro rates for a long time.

The first principal reason is that micro interest rates have been very, very supportive of share prices. Asking if low interest rates are good for stock prices is like asking if the Pope is Catholic. There is a very simple acronym that explains why this is so.

TINA. There Is No Alternative. Prior to 2008, stocks and bonds competed with each other for investors. If many portfolios had been historically geared as 60/40 stocks to bonds, that meant that at least 40% of all of the capital in the world, trillions and trillions of dollars, was allotted to bonds. The drastic reduction in interest rates made bonds much less appealing. This meant that an investor looking for anything better than a 2% return actually HAD to invest in stocks.

The TINA effect has resulted in some world-beating returns for stocks since 2009, when the new low interest rate regime really took hold. A simple investment in the S&P 500, a basket of stocks that represents the 500 largest companies in the world, would have delivered an annual return of 13.7%, for a total cumulative return of 312% in just eleven years. In other words, an investor would have turned $10,000 into $31,200 in the past eleven years.

Nothing wrong with that! Or is there? The problem with TINA is that it took choice away from investors. Investors come in all shapes and sizes, with all kinds of different goals, and when you take away options, you are forcing a lot of people into solutions that may not meet their needs. If you have been an aggressive stock market investor who focuses on share price, the last eleven years have been heaven. But if you are a more conservative investor looking to live off the wealth that you have accumulated with care and love over a lifetime, you have been living in hell.

Another way to think about the problem is by noting that, traditionally, investors fell into one of two general categories: investors who were still in accumulation phase, and investors who were in payout phase.

The traditional profile of an accumulator was someone who was still working every day in a job or business, and was interested in growing her savings as aggressively as possible. She would have been willing to take on more risk in exchange for that growth; after all, she was still working every day, so any temporary losses could still be made up through salary and/or active business earnings.

The payout phase investor was someone who now depended on those assets to pay her bills. Whether 45 or 75, the payout phase investor was, by her nature, more cautious and conservative. Because she didn't have an active day to day income, losing capital on risky investments would be more dangerous. These are traditionally the kind of investors who liked to buy safe, steady bonds at 6 or 7%.

At some point, the Greatest Generation faded away, and the Baby Boomers grabbed the wheel to guide society. And in case you haven't noticed, the Baby Boomers are not big on ageing gracefully, and never were into slow-but-steady anything. In fact, many of our most powerful business leaders today are in their 70s or even 80s! They will retire when they are dead; the more powerful or upwardly mobile they are, the more the Baby Boomers seem to want to work forever. So, many of today's "Super Seniors" are stuck in the accumulation phase. They are making more money in their 70s than they ever did. Too much is never enough, so they would never consider taking their foot off of the accelerator and converting their growing fortunes to less aggressive strategies. On a fundamental level, they don't understand the concept of sitting back and relaxing, so they have little regard for older people who are suffering today due to a dearth of traditional passive income options. This is the "Me" generation we are talking about here! If they have to put a gun to grandma's head and force her into the casino of stock market investing in order to make their own equities continue to rise, they will happily do so. The "Super Seniors" who you see leading the government and big business today have grown enormous stock market fortunes over the last eleven years, and they have no intention of letting anyone take away the punch bowl.

The second reason why I would foresee micro interest rates remaining for many years to come is even more scary: Uncle Sam is flat broke. Every year, the Federal Government must borrow more and more money to keep the lights on for the United States, and it is much easier to keep treading on thin ice if interest rates are very low.

Just how and when our national finances began to fray is a robust topic that easily could be a book, or several books, all on its own. In fact, I would recommend the work of Danielle DiMartino Booth. She spent substantial time working at the Federal Reserve, and she has written extensively on the topic of our proud nation's descent into voodoo economics. Suffice it to say, we have been living beyond our means for decades, and it's getting worse all the time. According to Thebalance.com, our national debt in 2008 was $5.8 trillion. By 2020, that debt had skyrocketed to $17.8 trillion! We certainly haven't felt broke during that time. In fact, public services have been mostly the same. As far as I know, we haven't seen any aircraft carriers hawked at garage sales and they haven't pawned the Liberty Bell yet. So how can these numbers work?

The Fed's black magic has been the only thing keeping us out of the poor house. Even though our debt has ballooned over time, our interest payments have barely changed at all. In 2008, our total interest payments due were $253 billion. In 2020, even though our national debt had tripled, our total interest payments were only $375 billion. In terms of our national budget, our interest service actually went down. In other words, in 2008, 8.5% of our national budget went towards interest payments. In 2020, even though our debt had tripled , we spent only 7.8% of our national budget on interest.

One heck of a neat trick, don't you think?

In economics jargon, this phenomenon is called "fiscal dominance." Basically, we may well see low interest rates for a long time, because the Federal Government can't pay its bills any other way. The Fed, the government body in charge of setting interest rates, is supposed to be deciding rates based on the "dual mandate." This refers to the dual goals of creating and protecting maximum employment for Americans while also maintaining stable prices. In reality, the Fed's low interest rates are the only thing standing between our nation and insolvency. It is going to take a jumbo sized black swan for interest rates to ever go back to "the good old days," when a conservative income investor could loan money to Uncle Sam and live off of the interest.

So now we have described the problem that today's passive income investor faces. We have explored the root causes just enough for you to understand some of the forces at work. Bonds haven't paid decent interest rates in years, and it seems highly unlikely that they will anytime soon. And yet, my rich private school friends haven't suddenly gotten jobs or sold the family jewels for income. Somehow they still get monthly or quarterly payments that provide income to pay all of their bills.

How?

Let's find out.

Chapter 2: Common Advice; Commonly Wrong

If there is one chapter of this book that could be considered the most important chapter, this would be it. The concept we are about to discuss can change your life.

It changed mine.

Two false statements separate millions of investors from the passive income they deserve.

Fallacy #1: Average dividends are 2-3%. If a stock pays much more than that, something is wrong.

Fallacy #2: Stocks with high dividends must be more risky. After all, more reward always comes with more risk.

Both of these statements are commonly believed, and not just by amateur investors. Many experienced financial advisors also believe these two statements. To be fair, they seem logical. But the logic is based on a profound misunderstanding about what goes on in corporate boardrooms across the United States.

The reason why these two statements are false is because corporate America is much more lucrative than most people realize. By now, you probably understand that I am not a fan of working in corporate America. But owning corporate America? Now that is another story entirely. Owning corporate America in the form of being a common shareholder is one of the greatest bonanzas in human history.

It turns out that most big name corporations only pay dividends between 1 and 3% because they feel like it. In fact, they could pay more cash to shareholders. Much more.

According to research done by Goldman Sachs, and cited in Barrons's magazine, in 2021, analysts expect the S&P 500 companies to pay out $524 billion in dividends. At the same time, Goldman Sachs expects the very same companies to buy back $602 billion of their own stock. In 2019, a bumper year before the coronavirus crisis, the S&P 500 companies actually bought back $750 billion of their own stock!

So, that "safe" corporation that is safe because it only has a 2% dividend? Turns out, it easily could have paid a 5% dividend. Instead, management chose to spend that money on share buybacks instead. That 3% yielder? Actually, it could have been 6%. Again, management chose not to pay out that much in cash dividends. And this doesn't even begin to take into account all of the money that was spent building corporate empires. According to statista.com, $3.9 trillion dollars changed hands in corporate mergers and acquisitions in 2019. If even a fraction of that money had been paid back to shareholders in dividends, rather than spent gobbling up other corporations, we could easily see dividends of 5% or more across the whole S&P 500.

But we don't. For some reason, corporate boards in the United States tend to think of dividends last when considering how to allot corporate funds. Why?

Dividends Vrs Stock Buybacks

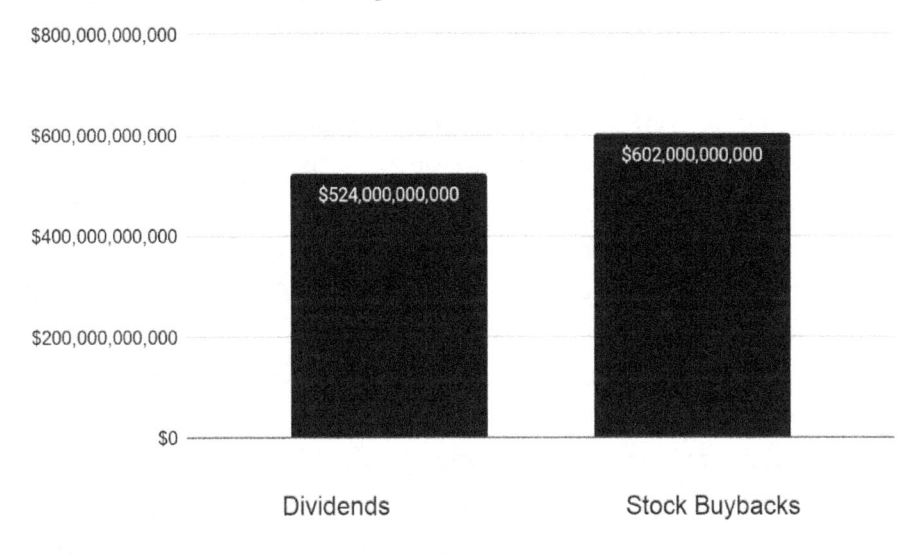

[Bar chart showing Dividends at $524,000,000,000 and Stock Buybacks at $602,000,000,000, with y-axis ranging from $0 to $800,000,000,000]

Figure 2

(Source, Goldman Sachs Estimate for 2021, as per Barron's Magazine)

The Rich Are Different From You and Me....

The way that corporate cash flow gets allocated simply comes down to priorities, and the priorities of the corporate Masters of the Universe are quite different from your average mom-and-pop investor.

Theoretically, each publicly traded corporation is overseen by a board of directors composed of shareholders. By law, a majority of the board members must be "independent" shareholders, meaning they hold a certain amount of shares as a passive investment and are not employed by the corporation they govern. The theory is that these people should have interests that are very similar to you and me.

The one thing that separates most S&P 500 corporate directors from you and me is that they are fabulously wealthy. I don't mean well to do, or upwardly mobile. I mean filthy stinking rich, tens or hundreds of millions of dollars rich. This changes their priorities whether they realize it or not.

Oceans of ink have been spilled over the growing gap between the "haves" and the "have nots" in America. It has been pointed out ad nauseum that the top 1% of Americans control an ever growing chunk of the economic pie. Most directors of large corporations are themselves highly accomplished executives, entrepreneurs, or ex-government officials. They have been chosen to direct the most complex, most prestigious corporations in the world based on their stellar record of prior corporate achievement. That means that most major corporations are being guided by people who have been in the 1% for years, if not decades.

It may seem counterintuitive, but the very rich in America do not seek to maximize their income. In fact, quite the opposite. Most very rich people in America spend substantial time and effort attempting to minimize income. Because in America, income means tax. Less income, less tax.

Try this thought exercise. Take a trip to fantasy island for a minute, and let's say your net worth is around $100,000,000, not an unusual achievement for today's high ranking corporate executives. Let's say that most of that net worth is in stocks. It's important to remember that even with that massive net worth, you are still employed. You get a paycheck in excess of $1,000,000 every year that pays for most of your needs. If you want an extra vacation home now and then, you simply cash in a million or two of stock and buy it. But mostly, your $100,0000,000 in net worth just sits there and grows, month by month, year by year. It's simply too much to reasonably spend, and you're not retired anyhow.

Let's look at three scenarios and think about which scenario you would favor if you were in this position. In scenario #1, your $100M is invested mostly in high yield dividend stocks, and you get about 6% in dividends every year. This means that your passive cash income from your investments is a massive $6,000,000 per year. You need to pay tax on that. Currently you would be looking at something in the range of 23% tax, so a cool $1.5 million would have to go to Uncle Sam. You're so rich it doesn't make a difference but....ouch! Who likes sending more than $1M to the feds?

In scenario #2, your $100M fortune is invested in a simple basket of S&P 500 stocks, which yield around 2% in cash dividends every year. So, in this case, you get $2M in passive cash every year and you pay about $450,000 in taxes. Still, ouch, but less ouch.

In scenario #3, your $100M fortune is invested primarily in high flying tech stocks and biotech stocks, most of which don't pay dividends. In this way, your fortune grows, on paper, as much as 12% per year. That amounts to $12,000,000 in paper profits each and every year. You get $0 in cash dividends, which means you pay $0 in tax every year. Your wealth grows by approximately $12,000,000 each and every year, and what you send to Uncle Sam is... nothing. Not bad, right?

Now, if you dare, multiply those numbers in your head by a factor of 10, or even a factor of 100. Many major corporations have directors and shareholders who would laugh at $100M. A lot of tech founders and executives have amassed fortunes well into the billions. What if those stocks paid hefty dividends? Who wants to pay tens, or even hundreds of millions, in tax?

So there you have it. The #1 reason why most major corporations in America pay only modest dividends is because the tycoons that run them don't want to pay tax on cash flow they don't need anyhow. Yes, they vaguely recognize that millions upon millions of small mom-and-pop investors could use enhanced dividends to pay for a modest existence. But most corporate directors are so rich that they live in their own world of wealth and privilege. Everyone they know wants lower income to pay less tax. Low corporate dividends are a symptom of our nation's growing wealth inequality.

Managers In Paradise

In theory, each public corporation is overseen by an independent board of directors who hold the c-suite accountable. In reality, many board members find it more profitable and easier to just go along with entrenched management. A lot of the largest corporations in America are run more for the benefit of the CEO than anybody else. In addition to the reasons discussed above, the c-suite may have a few distinct reasons for shunning dividends and choosing corporate buybacks instead.

Dividends are considered to be "sticky." This means that if a company runs into hard times, and has to cut its dividend, shareholders notice, immediately. If a corporation has paid a 3% dividend for many years, runs into some kind of problem, and is forced to cut that dividend, many long time shareholders will sell, and the stock price may start to fall. From the point of view of management, this makes the situation worse.

However, corporate share repurchases are sort of an invisible force. In theory, each share repurchase increases scarcity of shares, thus making each remaining share more valuable. In reality, there is only a fuzzy relationship between stock buybacks and share price. It's not like shares immediately increase in market value as soon as a buyback is completed. However, if a dividend is cut, the punishment in share price can be harsh and immediate.

Simply put, share buybacks are seen by most corporate managers as more low risk to them. If a dividend is cut, bad things start to happen immediately, and corporate managers can be blamed. Share buybacks are more flexible. Since their tangible benefit is mostly theoretical anyway, buybacks can be cut with few repercussions for management. How is that for twisted logic?

Another reason why some corporate managers choose stock buybacks over dividends is because they can use share buybacks to directly rig their pay packages. Many high level corporate executives earn multi-million-dollar bonuses based on a measure that is called "Per Share Earnings." This is the total earnings of the corporation, divided by the number of shares outstanding. So, if a company makes $100M and has 1 million shares outstanding on the market, then the earnings per share are $100. However, if the company makes the same $100M, and buys back 10% of its shares, then we divide $100M by only 900,000 outstanding shares. Shazam! Now the company earns $111.11 per share, even though the total earnings stayed the same. Cue massive bonus and third vacation property.

Why is this bit of financial chicanery allowed to happen in broad daylight? Remember, the CEO chooses the board of directors, and then the board of directors oversees the CEO. If that seems like an incestuous little arrangement, it is. But somehow corporate America hands in massive profits decade after decade, and share prices go up and up, so few people complain.

Speaking of massive profits: there is one last reason why many brand names and major corporations pay out much lower dividends than they could. They are so grotesquely profitable that they really don't need to draw any attention to the cozy racket they have set up. According to research done by Rakesh Shamra at Investopedia.com, the iPhone 7, which retailed for about $649 in 2016, cost about $5 in labor to assemble. Major corporations have piled up billions and billions in excess cash that is just sitting around, even after buying back countless billions of stock AND paying a dividend. If Apple paid out a 6% dividend, instead of its current 1% dividend, do you think people might start to wonder if they were paying too much for an iPhone?

Again, the people who make big decisions at Apple are so unfathomably wealthy that they will never spend the vast fortunes they have accumulated. So, given that cash flow is the last thing they need, why draw unneeded attention to the fact that they found a way to mint money by exploiting foreign labor? They would prefer to squirrel away hundreds of billions of dollars, which is what they have done, rather than drag it into the light where it could be scrutinized. Small dividends mean small transparency and small accountability for the corporate titans who reign over today's S&P 500 companies.

Saved By The Bell

You can think of the investing ecosystem like a high school. In that high school, the S&P 500 stocks represent "the cool kids." Rock stars like Tesla, Google, and Facebook are the center of all of the attention, and they set the tempo that everyone else moves to. But if you ever went to high school, you know that there are all kinds of other cliques, many of which provide unique value. You had the drama kids, the band nerds, and the technogeeks. You had the grade grubbers, the stoners, and the foreign exchange students. If there is one lesson that many of us learned as the years have gone by, it's that a lot of those less popular kids have done just fine as they have gone out into the world.

I am going to teach you to do just fine by ignoring what the cool kids are doing and looking for value in other parts of the equity ecosystem. The S&P 500 is just one subset of publicly traded companies. In reality, there are thousands of different investments to choose from.

Stocks that pay high dividends are not necessarily dangerous, and there may not be anything wrong with them at all. They're just poorly understood, like that computer nerd back in high school who is a tech billionaire today. He was overlooked in high school because he thought differently than others, and he didn't give a flip about what the cool kids were doing. But anyone with a discerning eye back then would have known that shunned kid was going somewhere.

How can we gain a discerning eye? How do we identify value? How do we figure out which stocks will keep pumping out passive income forever, and which ones are duds?

In the next chapter we will begin to build your research toolkit, so you can find the answers to these investment questions and reap the corresponding profits.

Chapter 3: Fallen Angels

The first way to look for exceptional dividend stocks is to find the ones that are hiding in plain sight. These are a group of stocks that I call "fallen angels": Well-known companies who have a high dividend yield because they have fallen out of favor. When a stock becomes unpopular, its share price can fall, even though the underlying business still generates plenty of free cash flow. This can lead to a situation where a stock that used to yield 2% now yields 4%, or a stock that used to yield 3% now yields 6%. The math works like this. If your shares trade at $10, and pay a $0.25 dividend, then your dividend yield is 2.5%. Very average. But if your share price falls to $5, and you still pay the same $0.25 dividend, all of the sudden your stock boasts a 5% dividend. Better than average. Of course, if you owned the stock at $10, and now it's worth $5, you won't be happy. But if you find the stock after the fall, when it's trading at just $5 and paying a meaty 5% dividend, you may well have just found yourself a deal.

Sometimes, these former belles of the ball have been eschewed for a good reason. Maybe something is wrong in their industry or with their specific product. Often, they simply sell a product or service that has gone out of style with Wall Street.

Was there anything wrong with those Z-Cavaricci pants that you used to wear with pride to the best parties? No, they worked just fine. At some point, however, you stopped wearing them because everyone else did. They just went out of style. That is what happens with a "fallen angel stock.

GILEAD SCIENCES: A Case Study

As I write this, one excellent example of a fallen angel is Gilead Sciences. Over the last five years, Gilead's share price has slumped from $100 per share to just $58 per share. For reference, the S&P 500 returned a total of 97% for those same five years. So, if you had bought almost any other stock, you could have doubled your money in five years. If you bought Gilead, you actually cut your money in half. Wow! This must really be a company in trouble, right?

Not really. In 2019, as the company's shares plumbed all new lows, Gilead still produced $9 billion in positive cash flow! In fact, that $9 billion was more than the previous year's positive cash flow of $8.4 billion. The company had $24 billion in cash just laying around, and only very modest debt at very low interest rates.

As Gilead has seen its share price shrivel, the dividend has only gone UP. In 2015, the biotech firm paid roughly a 1.5% dividend. As of 2020, that dividend has approached 5%. This huge rise in the dividend yield has happened for two reasons. First, as the share price has fallen, even if management had only maintained the same dividend, the dividend yield would have grown as a percentage. However, management did not just hold the dividend steady. They actually grew the dividend reliably, year after year. In 2015, the dividend was $0.43 per share per quarter, and today that dividend stands at $0.68 per share per quarter.

Many investors, even professional investors, see this kind of situation and immediately take a pass. If a company has faced headwinds, and the stock price has fallen, but the dividend has actually gone up, they assume that the company is paying out money it doesn't have in order to keep investors from abandoning ship. The assumption is that a desperate company is paying out whatever it can now, sacrificing future growth by paying out cash that it shouldn't. Sometimes that is the case. But often, it isn't, and that is where the opportunity comes in.

While Gilead's revenue has gone in the wrong direction over the last few years, the core business is still a prodigious cash generation machine, and we can see that Gilead can afford it's dividend raises with ease. In 2019, the business generated $9.1 billion in free cash flow, but only paid out $3.2 billion as a dividend. Over the years between 2015 and 2020, while Gilead was busy hiking its dividend, the company invested an average of $4 billion a year in research and development, and ended the period with a massive $24 billion cash balance in its bank account. A company with a constantly rising dividend, a constantly rising bank account, and a steady commitment to investment in research and development. Does this sound like a sinking ship to you?

So why was the share price punished so viciously over the last few years? Poor Gilead just got its story wrong. Perhaps you have heard the phrase "story stock?" An example of a story stock would be Tesla. A charismatic founder, a clear mission to save the world, legions of nerdy fans. Wall Street has paid little attention to the mathematical fundamentals of Tesla, because the story is just so compelling. Gilead used to be the Tesla of biotech, until, one day, it wasn't. Turns out that pundits and fanboys who fall in love with a stock can just as easily turn sour. If you have ever experienced a love affair gone bad, you may know the feeling.

Gilead's original claim to fame was that they pioneered the first effective treatment for HIV. If you lived through the 80s and 90s, you know that HIV had an all pervasive effect on the global cultural conversation, in the same way climate change does today. Gilead rocketed from obscurity to dazzling fame by taking a dagger to the heart of the boogeyman who haunted millions of nightmares around the globe.

Gilead didn't cure HIV, but they did get the epidemic under control by creating a medical regimen that has helped millions of patients live healthy lives for decades. For their next trick, they aimed even bigger. No more indefinite treatments. Gilead was aiming to use their hard-earned scientific knowledge to slay some viruses, once and for all.

Amazingly, they did. Starting in 2013, Gilead found a way to cure hepatitis C. Although not as visible as HIV had been, the Center for Disease Control estimated that formerly incurable hepatitis C killed as many as 19,659 Americans per year by 2014; that's more than all other infectious diseases combined.

Gilead had an instant phenomena on its hands; revenue and profit skyrocketed overnight. So did the share price. The value of the company quadrupled in just a few years.

In one of the more cruel ironies in the annals of American business history, Gilead cured its way into a stock crash. It's hepatitis C treatment has been so effective that less and less people contract and spread hepatitis. According to the CDC's National Progress Report on Hepatitis C, the mortality rate of the disease had dropped from 5 per 100,000 Americans to 3.72 per 100,000 Americans just between 2013 and 2018, with the trend pointing to further declines heading into the 2020s. Great news for patients. Great news for humanity. Terrible news for Gilead.

The result at Gilead was falling revenue. Just as the company had enjoyed a massive boom in revenue from 2013 to 2015, they have endured a slow but steady decline as their own medical breakthrough has brought America's hepatitis C epidemic under control. Talk about a victim of your own success!

The important thing to remember in this case study is that Gilead still makes money. A lot of money. Gilead still has cash on hand. A lot of cash on hand. And Gilead still pays great dividends. Lately, Gilead has decided to deploy these impressive resources in the quest to reignite growth. They have brought in a new CEO and made a string of big name acquisitions. It may take years for them to return to the glory of their hepatitis C days. But in the meantime, that dividend just keeps growing.

Gilead was kicked out of investing heaven because their profit and loss statement, prepared under Generally Accepted Accounting Principles (GAAP), no longer told the sexy biotech growth story that many impatient investors demand. However, Gilead's rock solid cash flow and balance sheet tell a different story. It's this chasm between theoretical accounting for growth and real world accounting for cash flow where the skilful dividend investor finds the best opportunities. We will go over this technique in more detail at the end of the chapter, but just remember the following principle: while everyone else is running out the door in a stampede, you just remember to double check and see if they dropped anything of value. Sometimes in their panic to move their money to the latest hot stock, they leave some juicy dividends ripe for the taking.

Sectors In Exile

In the case study above, we explored one particular stock with specific problems that have led it to be shunned by investors who have missed the value that lies just under the surface.

However, it's not uncommon for entire sectors to fall out of favor. Traditional Wall Street analysts are very big on categorizing stocks so that they can compare "like" with "like" companies. One reason for this is because in an apples-to-apples comparison, all of the inputs and outputs are theoretically the same for all of the players, therefore analysts can focus on a narrow set of factors that might differentiate one company from another. For example, Wall Street analysts would typically group all gold mining companies together. The theory would be that they all have similar raw inputs (there is the same amount of gold in the world for everyone to discover) and similar outputs (gold demand is the same for every seller of gold….gold demand is global). Therefore, if company X did better than company Y, it would mean that company X had better management, or better partners.

While these kinds of groupings may make life easier for Wall Street, they often lead to a phenomenon where entire sectors fall out of favor all at once. If the fundamentals of a sector no longer seem appealing, then all of the companies in that bucket are just ignored. Sometimes whole sectors should be ignored. But often, the fact that an entire sector comprised of dozens of companies has been painted with the same brush means opportunity for the astute investor.

One example of a sector that is currently on the outs' is oil. This may be an example of a sector that has fallen out of favor for some good reasons. Some people won't touch oil due to moral concerns related to climate change. Others feel that oil is simply yesterday's resource. Either way, it has led to a situation where massive international energy corporations are selling for dirt cheap. At some point during 2020, Exxon Mobil, one of the largest energy companies in the world, had seen it's share price drop so far that it was yielding 10%! Exxon, like all oil companies, had a terrible 2020 as the coronavirus created historic turmoil in the energy markets. Exxon may struggle as we move through the 21st century and renewable energy becomes dominant. However, according to Industr.com, there are currently 2,000,000,000 internal combustion engines on the road, and, as of today, 95% of new vehicles still need gas. The oil industry will continue to churn out cash flow for many years to come, and may be a suitable investment for a senior citizen who isn't overly concerned about climate change. A reliable 10% yield from Exxon Mobil would go a long way towards helping grandma squeeze a decent income from a modest nest egg.

Another example of an industry that has been left for dead is the tobacco industry. As the link between tobacco and cancer has been more and more firmly established, smoking rates have plummeted, which you would think would have made tobacco a terrible investment. You would be wrong. The corporate scoundrels who run Altria, one of the world's largest tobacco companies, found a way to produce $4.9 billion in free cash flow in just the first six months of 2020, a time period that witnessed one of the worst economic contractions in history. Of that, Altria pays out a whopping 77%, leaving the stock with a massive 8% dividend. You might have very good reasons to stay away from investments in tobacco, but the sure death of the tobacco industry shouldn't be one of them. If Altria could produce bountiful cash flow during one of the worst economic crises of the last 100 years, you can be sure that the earnings are more than just smoke and mirrors.

So you might understand why an industry that profits by accelerating death might have fallen from grace in the investment community. But what about an industry dedicated to preserving life? The pharmaceutical industry, or Big Pharma, is a classic example of a sector that has gone in and out of style dozens of times over the decades. Often accused of exploiting the vulnerable through questionable pricing practices, in 2020 Big Pharma was America's knight in shining armor, delivering a raft of coronavirus treatments in record time. Based on Big Pharma's heroic performance during our time of national crisis, suddenly the industry was invited back into the country club of "hot" sectors. But this hasn't always been the case.

As recently as 2018, the Wall Street Journal published an article entitled, "What is Ailing the Drug Industry?" (June 22, 2018). The WSJ described Big Pharma as the definition of an out of fashion industry:

> *U.S. health-care spending regularly grows faster than inflation and has reached about 18% of gross domestic product. Prescription drugs are a major component of that sum. The Centers for Medicare and Medicaid Services projects that total U.S. drug spending will rise by 68% to $600 billion by 2026. Meanwhile, the Food and Drug Administration is approving new medicines at a brisk rate and venture capitalists have poured billions into biotech startups.*
>
> *Yet the stock market is treating drugmakers as a struggling industry. The NYSE Arca Pharmaceutical Index has underperformed the S&P 500 by nearly 30 percentage points over the past two years. Not all drug companies are suffering. Over that same time frame, an index of small biotech stocks has beaten the S&P 500 by more than 50 percentage points.*

You may notice in the quotation above that the WSJ took pains to point out that not all components of the drug industry were underperforming. In fact, biotech, a risky sub-sector famous for a casino-like ethos, was booming. Society was spending on medicines at a growing rate. But big, established pharmaceutical companies like Pfizer, Eli Lilly, and Johnson&Johnson were left out in the cold, like a bunch of nerds refused entrance to the hottest dance club in town.

The Wall Street Journal went on to offer all kinds of theories as to why biotech was piling up high returns while it's more mature cousin, Big Pharma, languished. But the real reason was a lack of sex appeal. As time goes by, memories of the Trump years may start to fade. But when the host of The Apprentice swept into Washington like a tornado, it awakened what many commentators call "the animal spirits," the idea that any risk is a good risk, and the sky's the limit. The early Trump years were what analysts call a "risk on environment." Unprofitable young biotech companies with big futures just seemed a lot more alluring than stodgy, established Big Pharma companies with a century of dividend paying credentials under their belt.

This mismatch between what was in style in 2016 and what would meet the needs of an income-oriented investor meant a huge opportunity. Many brand name pharmaceutical stocks, which had been reliably pumping out dividends for decades, could be purchased with a dividend yield between 4 and 6%. Compare that to 2% on most bonds. In the "Go Go" beginning of the Trump era, Big Pharma was the dowdy older sister who wasn't invited to the party. But contrarian dividend hunters found plenty to value, and today they enjoy plentiful dividends that show up like clockwork every three months.

Accounting and You

This is the part of the book where I dispense some unpopular advice. If you want to be able to identify the best fallen angel opportunities for yourself, you need to learn some basic accounting. This is advice coming from a guy who was a mediocre math student who never made it past basic algebra in school. In fact, accounting is less like a complicated math discipline and more like a language. Maybe you are slapping your forehead with your hand and groaning right now; maybe you struggled through two years of high school French and quit. Learning a language, even the language of business, is not popular for most people. But it may not be as hard as you imagine. Think of the example of Martin Luther.

You may remember from history class or religious school that Martin Luther was the founder of Protestant Christianity in the 16th century. Luther's ideas upset a lot of the Powers that Were, and as such, he spent a lot of time in jail. How do you pass the time if you are stuck in a hellish, medieval jail filled with rats and plague? If you are the founder of a major world religious movement, you study religion. In Luther's time, that meant studying in Latin, Ancient Greek, and Hebrew. His native language was German. I remember being dazzled at the revelation. How on earth would a 16th century German have mastered languages that had been dead for a thousand years? In an era when most people couldn't read at all, how was pious Martin Luther mastering three different obscure languages from his jail cell?

It turns out that Luther, and religious scholars like him, only had to learn a very limited form of each language. Luther learned to study biblical texts in their original languages, but he wasn't about to start having long conversations in Ancient Greek with his German cellmates. Luther only needed to understand these languages in certain, very specific contexts, contexts that are mostly fixed and predictable. Learning the language of accounting would be the same for an income-oriented investor.

You don't need to earn an accounting degree or become a Certified Public Accountant. To find the best fallen angel investment opportunities, you just need to learn to identify certain specific numerical situations.

One example of these kinds of opportunities is the dichotomy that often exists between a company's accrual accounting and its cash accounting. By law, each publicly traded company must publish a profit and loss statement, which is governed by the rules of accrual accounting, and a cash flow statement, which is governed by cash accounting. The company must also publish a balance sheet statement, which is a summary of the company's assets and liabilities at a particular moment in time.

Accrual accounting is a kind of accounting that factors in theoretical costs and revenues, and gives tangible numbers to intangible concepts. For example, if your company hands out a billion dollars in stock options, that is noted as an expense in the accrual accounting of the profit and loss statement. That $1 billion in stock options cost the company $0 in actual cash out the door, but by law it still shows up as an expense in the profit and loss (P&L).

The cash flow statement only factors in the tangible cash that goes out and comes into the business. If you were running a lemonade stand as a kid, you were concerned with the cash flow statement. You factored in the money you put in, you factored in the money you took out, and if you took out more than you put in, you were making money.

The opportunity arises because 90% of investors only pay attention to the P&L statement. The P&L statement is what grabs all of the headlines in the financial media. A shocking number of growth stocks somehow manage a soaring share price with no cash flow at all. The fantasy world of the P&L statement can have a very real effect on share price. You are looking for the instances where the share price crashes because of an unattractive P&L, even though the cash flow revealed on the cash flow statement remains hearty.

Let's circle back to the example of Gilead that we discussed earlier. From a P&L perspective, Gilead looked bad. Revenue went down a few years in a row. That is the headline that the world saw. But remember what we found when we dug a little deeper and we scrutinized the cash flows? We found a company that was still minting money like clockwork. We found a company that could easily maintain its hefty dividend while still reinvesting back into the business. All of this bounty was lost on investors who only focused on the P&L statement.

If you take a basic accounting class, available for free or cheap online, or you read *Accounting for Dummies*, you will already be ahead of 90% of investors. Investing in fallen angels is all about finding opportunities that others have missed. The reward is a lucrative, income-producing equity that you bought on sale.

Chapter 4: Dividend Growth Investing

A lot of people view dividend stocks as a way to preserve wealth. A way to gain safe and regular income from wealth that has already been accumulated. But did you know that income stocks can also be an effective way to get rich? Although many dividend stocks lack the panache and media buzz of "growth" stocks such as big technology names, there is a method of dividend investing that can help you grow your wealth at an exponential rate.

This method is referred to as "dividend growth investing." The idea may seem counterintuitive at first, but some basic arithmetic reveals the awesome compounding power of boring stocks.

The basic concept is the following: don't focus on stocks with the highest dividend yields, focus on stocks that grow their dividend at a very high and sustained rate. In other words, don't worry about scoring a stock that currently yields 10%. Rather, focus on finding a stock with a modest dividend yield that is growing at an annual rate of 10%.

This methodology is recommended for anyone who will measure their retirement in decades rather than years. If you are a 75-year-old retiree, you would probably be better off just choosing stocks that have high dividend yields now. However, if you have just quit your corporate career at age 45, and want to live off your dividend income for decades to come, dividend growth investing makes sense for you. Dividend growth investing is also a recommendable technique for people who either can't or don't want to do a lot of research. This is a very popular method, so it's easy to find lists online of brand name stocks that grow their dividend rapidly.

Simple Math. Shocking Math.

As I mentioned earlier, I was never great at math in school. But even some basic arithmetic can demonstrate the amazing outcomes that are possible through dividend growth investing.

To start with, let's ask ourselves the following: what constitutes above average dividend growth? Wyo Investments recently published a piece on this topic on the website Seeking Alpha. The author is a young retiree with eleven years of dividend growth investment under his belt. Here is his criteria for "high dividend growth. "My current goal is twofold; Maintain 7% dividend growth without reinvesting dividends. Achieve 10% dividend growth with reinvesting dividends." (Seeking Alpha, 1/5/21). The author goes on to list a portfolio of 40 stocks, many of which are household names, that have met that criteria.

What has been the practical implications of that growth? Between the years 2016 and 2021, his overall dividend income increased from $8,000 per year to $12,500 per year. That is without him investing any additional capital; sometimes he spent his dividends, sometimes he reinvested them. Either way, he grew his passive income by over 50% in just five years. How many of you have gotten a 50% raise at your job over just five years?

Another way of thinking of the growth potential is simply to compare your rate of dividend growth to the rate of inflation. During the time period referenced above, inflation hovered somewhere around 2% annually. That means that Wyo Investments easily found investments with passive income streams that grew at four times the rate of inflation. You can see the powerful results achieved in just five years. What would the results look like over longer periods of time?

I'd Like To Buy The World a Coke

Typically when we think of millionaire-maker stocks, we imagine high flying growth stocks like Tesla, Google, or some biotech firm. But what if I told you that you walk by liquid gold every time you go to your grocery store? Plain, old, boring Coca-Cola has made a mind boggling fortune for Warren Buffett and many other investors.

Before we go into the specific math of Coca-Cola, we need to discuss a key vocabulary lesson. Typically, when we are talking about income producing stocks, the term used to discuss the current dividend is "dividend yield." This is a percentage-based measure of how much the current dividend is. So, for example, if company X has a share price $10, and is paying a $0.50 annual dividend, then company X currently has a dividend yield of 5%.

But the key concept to remember is that dividend yield is a fluid measurement that changes with market conditions over time. Your costs do not. So, if company X's share price slowly rises to $20 over time, and the dividend slowly rises to $1 as well, then your current dividend yield remains 5%. But you bought the stock at $10 years ago. Now the dividend has risen to $1 per year. That means that your base cost has stayed the same, and your yield has doubled. So, your current dividend yield is 5%, but your "yield to cost" is a whopping 10%. This is the secret formula that makes boring companies like Coke so lucrative over time.

Author Sean Williams explained how Buffett has profited immensely from his long term investments in Coke and American Express:

Buffett also holds true to his winners. For instance, Coca-Cola has been a Berkshire Hathaway holding for more than three decades, while American Express has been a consistent holding for more than 25 years. As these two companies have appreciated in value and grown their payouts over time, Berkshire's annual yield based on the original cost basis for Coca-Cola and American Express has soared. Paying out almost $261 million annually, yet with a cost basis of only $1.287 billion, AmEx is providing a roughly 20% yield each year. Meanwhile, Coca-Cola's $656 million in annual dividends, relative to its $1.299 billion cost basis, means it provides a 50.5% yield from its initial cost basis every year. (Fool.com, 3/5/20)

Boring old Coca-Cola has made a fortune for Warren Buffet. It can do the same for you.

Yield to Cost, Illustrated

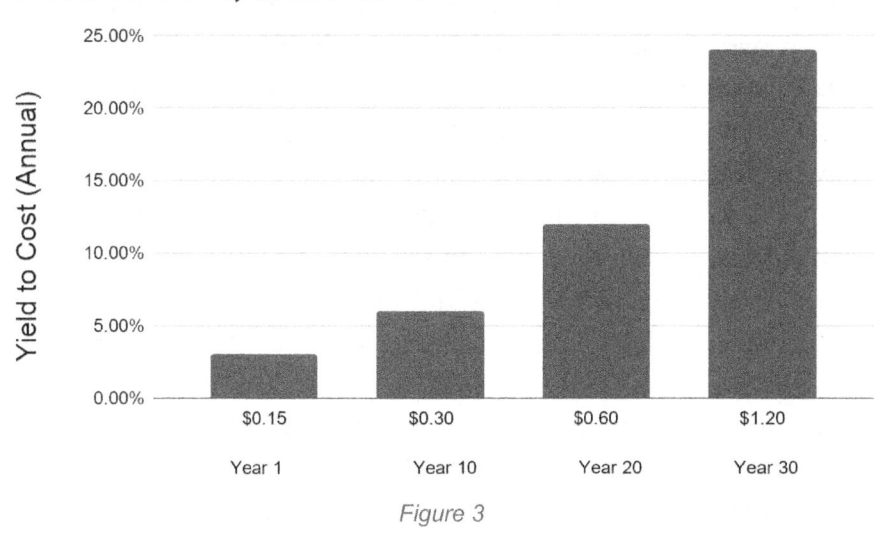

Figure 3

You buy shares in a theoretical company at $5. Even if they raise the dividend by 7% annually, the cost you paid for those shares will always remain fixed. Thus, your "Yield to Cost" as a percentage just goes up year after year, no matter how big the dividend grows. Although not pictured in this illustration, the investor likely benefited from share price appreciation as well, which would further boost overall returns.

Money For Nuthin' and Divs For Free

Perhaps the best thing about dividend growth investment is that it's uncommonly easy. If you found the search for fallen angel stocks to be intimidating and exhausting, then the relative ease of dividend growth investing may appeal to you.

A great place to start shopping for dividend growth is the "dividend aristocrats." A company is dubbed a dividend aristocrat if it has grown its dividend every single year for 25 consecutive years. Think about all of the challenges that have arisen over the last 25 years! The tech bubble crash, 9/11, the Great Recession. For 64 very special publicly traded firms, all of these blows barely put a dent in their armor. They just kept paying more and more no matter what was going on in society.

According to Moneyinvestexpert.com, amongst these 64 companies, the average dividend growth rate was 6% annually, or three times the rate of inflation. But that was just the average. Of the 64 dividend aristocrats, the top had often grown their dividends at an annual rate of 12% or more over the last decade. That means that these "boring" companies doubled their dividend payout every six years! Have you ever had a job where you could double your salary every six years for decades on end?

It's easy to identify great stocks for your dividend growth portfolio. Just Google "dividend aristocrats" and "dividend growth rate" or "DGR" and numerous lists will appear.

If you don't even want to do that, you can easily harness the power of dividend growth investing through exchange traded funds. Here is a list of five different exchange traded funds that will help you harness the power of dividend growth without ever losing a night's sleep (from Investopedia.com):

- ProShares S&P 500 Dividend Aristocrats ETF (NOBL)
- ProShares S&P Technology Dividend Aristocrats ETF (TDV)
- SPDR S&P Dividend ETF (SDY)
- SPDR S&P Global Dividend ETF (WDIV)
- ProShares S&P MidCap 400 Dividend Aristocrats ETF (REGL)

This is a powerful strategy considering the small amount of effort required. If you had bought one of the more established exchange traded funds above, SDY, in 2010, you would have turned $46 into $109 even if you spent the dividend every year. If you invest in dividend aristocrats and hold onto these stocks through thick and thin, you will be the one who winds up feeling like a king.

Chapter 5: European Stocks

Ah, Europe, sweet Europe. French baguettes and Spanish tapas. Beer and wine ripened in the Old World sun. Six-week vacations. Certainly a continent known for easy living and a penchant for the high life.

But did you know that it's also easy to find high dividend paying stocks in Europe? This doesn't require special knowledge, or even much work at all. Many Euro stocks simply pay higher dividends than their American equivalents. For example, the EuroStoxx 50, a broad index of the fifty largest European companies, has paid a median divided yield of 3% over the last five years; at times that yield has gone as high as 4.22%. By comparison, the S&P 500 in America has typically yielded around 1.8% during the same time period. With no skill at all, you could earn double the dividend yield of American stocks just by buying a European exchange traded fund.

Many critics could say that companies that pay "too much" dividend are not growing. They say something must be wrong if they pay double the dividend of their American competitors. This is a wrongheaded notion. Remember the math we went over in earlier chapters. Most major American companies have enough cash flow that they could easily pay much higher dividends. They choose not to. Instead, they typically choose to buy back their own stock. Europeans prefer plain old dividends.

Math is math, and greed is greed. History shows that all human beings, whether they be from Philadelphia or Flanders, like to get paid. So why would Europeans choose to receive payment in the form of dividends rather than share buybacks?

A different history and a different culture lead to different choices. Let's take a look at three reasons why European capitalists prefer dividends.

The Noble Dividend

One of the most important reasons why large, publicly traded European companies tend to reward shareholders with dividends rather than buybacks is the ownership structure. Many large, brand-name Euro companies are actually still controlled by founding families. This arrangement would NOT be like Walmart now, which is controlled by Sam Walton's four children. This would be like Walmart circa the year 2100, when it is controlled by Sam Walton's 25 great grandchildren.

In the Old World, everything is, well, old. So, large, well-known corporations that have been in business for hundreds of years are still controlled by families. Because it's been so many generations, the family shareholdings themselves are often split between dozens of cousins, which, as you can imagine, can lead to some migraine-inducing ownership structures.

One example would be Roche. Roche is a global pharmaceutical giant with around 95,000 employees. The company was founded in Basel, Switzerland in 1896, and is still domiciled in Switzerland. The total value of the company's shares on the open market is $300,000,000,000, of which half are still owned by dozens of cousins descendent from the founding Hoffmann family.

So, a private family still controls the third largest pharmaceutical company in the world. Nice work if you can get it. The way they got it was by never selling shares. Roche has shunned share buybacks in comparison to it's American counterparts because selling shares would not be in the interest of the controlling family. The only way that share buybacks work is if someone wants to sell shares. The members of the Hoffmann family haven't sold in over a century.

In the world of Euro stocks, selling shares means selling control for some very, very rich families. So, dividends become the preferred method of rewarding shareholders. According to moneyinvestexpert.com, Roche has raised the dividend for 32 consecutive years. Every shareholder gets the same dividend payout, whether you are a member of the Hoffmann family, or just a plain Deiter in the cobblestoned street. That annual cash payout has quintupled since the year 2000. As I write this, the current share price is $43 and the dividend yield is 1.7%. But remember, the Hoffmann family has owned the same shares since they were worth just $4 or less. So they could easily be reaping a 20% annual yield to cost, or even much more. Who needs the aggravation of share buybacks? Meaty dividends have funded a regal lifestyle for Roche's controlling shareholders for the last century.

Another reason why founding families would be reluctant to dilute their corporate control by selling is because of who their other shareholders are. In Europe, most major companies have several large blocks of shareholders. In Germany, for example, by law labor unions must have a certain percentage of representation on the board of directors. At the same time, it's not uncommon for local or even national governments to own a large block of shares. So, a controlling family that sells shares to get quick cash risks handing corporate control to the labor unions, or worse still, the government.

Due to these baroque shareholder structures, founding families are often in a tug-of-war with other large shareholders. Lately, this has been a very hot topic at Volkswagen, the largest manufacturer of cars in the world. On the company's website, the Board of Directors is described as the following: "The Supervisory Board of Volkswagen AG comprises 20 members and conforms to the German Co-determination Act." This means that, by law, labor unions must be represented on the board. The State of Lower Saxony owns 20% of the company, so the government has representatives on the board. The government of Qatar owns 17% of the company, so they have representatives on the board. The founding family owns 35% of the company, but controls 50% of the votes due to special share classes, so they have representatives on the board. The unwieldy nature of this ownership structure was laid bare in 2020, as the industry wide shift to electrification caused private power struggles to burst into into the open:

> *FRANKFURT, Nov 27 (Reuters) - Volkswagen's Chief Executive Herbert Diess has asked the company's owning families to back a contract extension in a bid to break a management deadlock at the world's largest carmaker, two people familiar with the matter told Reuters.*
>
> *The appeal for support from the Piech and Porsche families, who control a majority voting stake at the carmaker, comes after Diess was forced to relinquish management responsibility for the VW brand in June to retain his job as group CEO.*
>
> *"He is bringing the issue to a head," one of the sources said.*
>
> *Volkswagen declined to comment. The owning families declined to comment, the company's works council and the German state of Lower Saxony, which owns a VW stake, declined to comment.*

To American investors, this scenario seems bizarre, but it's a common situation on the European continent: at some of the world's largest, best-known companies, it's hard to tell who's really in charge. If you were a member of a controlling family, and you were legally forced into a constant, uncomfortable tango with labor unions and the government, would you want to sell shares? Does it look like anyone at Volkswagen wants to give up an ounce of control? In these kinds of situations, steady and growing dividends are the way that shareholders can reap cash flow without ceding control.

Speaking of uncomfortable, isn't it surprising to learn that Europe, a continent now renowned for a socialsitic way of life, is still home to many mega corporations that are still controlled by what is essentially aristocracy? How can a continent that taxes workers' incomes at up to 60% still be home to Lords and Ladies who have owned major corporations through passive vehicles for a century or more? How is France, the home of "Liberte, Egalite and Fraternite" also the home of Bernard Arnault, a world-famous billionaire whose family controls publicly traded LVMH-Moet-Hennesy, the legendary purveyor of luxury goods?

The answers to these questions are beyond the scope of this book, but suffice it to say that big business in Europe struggles with dicey publicity. They wouldn't want to attract the negative attention that big share buybacks can bring in America.

When a company is swimming in cash, many observers feel that share buybacks hurt workers and "stakeholders", i.e. people who depend on the company for their livelihoods, even if they aren't shareholders. For example, cash burned on share buybacks could instead be invested in factories that create new jobs, or invested in cleaning up a company's environmental footprint. In America, the cultural attitude that prevails is that companies exist to build wealth for shareholders alone; lip service is provided for other stakeholders, but when push comes to shove, American culture is all about getting paid.

Many Europeans may secretly feel the same way, but the prevailing culture is very focused on fairness and social well being. The fact that France taxes workers at double American rates, yet also provides Dior and Hermes luxuries to the world, is just a careful balancing act that corporations must navigate. In this environment, the quiet regularity of dividends draws less negative attention than share buybacks.

We're All Euro Now

Studies show that many investors suffer from what researchers call "home country bias." This means that Americans are more comfortable buying American stocks, Japanese more comfortable buying Japanese stocks, etc. While there are many great reasons to accumulate American stocks (which we will go over in the following chapters), some allotment to European stocks is recommendable if you want to live off of dividend payments.

Some investors hesitate to purchase European stocks due to technical concerns. Maybe this would have been a barrier thirty years ago, but today it's very easy. Whatever brokerage you use in America is likely to offer a wide variety of ADRs from major companies all over God's Green Earth. An ADR is an American Depository Receipt. It is a ticker symbol that trades on American stock exchanges mirroring the share listing of stock in its home country. I own dozens of ADRs; they are just as easy to buy as an American stock.

Another rational concern might be accounting and standards. Most Americans are familiar with financial regulatory bodies like the SEC (Securities Exchange Commission) and the IRS. How can we trust stocks from foreign lands? What if the accounting is different, adding complexity? Is anyone regulating these stocks at all?

The good news is that the very rich people who own the majority of stocks are typically citizens of the world. They often travel widely and own assets on every continent. As such, you can usually expect similar standards in accounting and financial regulation across major global financial markets. Would I recommend buying stocks based in Latvia? Perhaps not. But core, Western European countries have been doing this a long, long time. You can expect accounting and financial rules to be similar to what you would find on this side of the Atlantic. Regulatory documents will almost always be available published in English.

Some investors who pay attention to current affairs and global economics might have one last, common sense question. If European economic growth is sluggish, why would an American want to invest in European stocks?

It's been well documented that European economic growth has been sub-par for many years. Double digit unemployment is common in the southern half of the EU, the birth rate is the lowest it's ever been, and growth of Gross Domestic Product has been anemic for most of the 21st century. If European companies only sold goods in Europe, I would tell you not to invest.

However, that very sluggishness is what has caused long established European large capitalization companies to become global powerhouses. VW, despite it's chronically dysfunctional ownership structure, remains the largest car manufacturer by volume in the world. They certainly didn't sell all of those cars in Germany! VW has operations in almost every country on the map. Wherever growth is on the globe, VW is there. The same goes for Roche, and most other companies that make up the Euro Stoxx 50.

The only reason we categorize these companies as "European" is because a disproportionate number of shareholders and upper management are European citizens. This leads to decisions that can be different than companies primarily owned by Americans; for instance, the decision to pay out dividends rather than buy back stock. But make no mistake; these titans of global commerce do business in any country that has a solvent currency. As a shareholder, we simply sit back, relax, and enjoy our quarterly dividend checks. How to make those dividend checks grow is the problem of Claus or Francois back at headquarters.

How To Choose

How to find good dividend stocks headquartered in the Old World? The process is very simple. 90% of Americans don't even bother to look across the pond due to that home country bias phenomenon. Just by looking, you can instantly beat out 90% of your competitors.

If you don't want to put in the time and effort to do research, you can always buy a broad based exchange traded fund, just like the Euro Stoxx 50 that we discussed earlier in the chapter. Pretty much every flavor of American exchange traded fund has a European equivalent, which can easily be procured from companies like Vanguard or iShares. Very often, these ETFs will yield more than their American counterparts, because of all the reasons we reviewed earlier in the chapter.

Even if you prefer individual shares, the process can be simple. In the next few chapters, we will be reviewing different industry sectors in the American stock market that tend to offer high yields. If you decide, for example, that you want to invest in oil, first check American companies. Then look up European counterparts. For example, as I write this text, Chevron, a legendary American oil company, offers a dividend yield of 5.6%. BP (British Petroleum) has nearly identical operations across the globe, but offers a dividend yield of 7.67%. These two companies aren't clones, but in reality they are very similar. One yields 30% more than the other. Making the trip across the Atlantic may well be worth it.

You can repeat this comparison in most major sectors. Energy, pharmaceuticals, consumer goods, even real estate investment trusts. Comparing European companies to American companies is just like checking out both Amazon.com and Walmart.com before you buy. Good shoppers find good deals. So can you.

Why do both Europe and America host mega corporations that compete over the very same markets globally? Because some businesses are so good, that everyone wants in. In the next chapters we will review two businesses that you, too, may want to own.

Chapter 6: Big Pharma, Big Dividends

If you want secure and growing dividends, then the pharmaceutical industry offers the good medicine you seek. In the good old days that we discussed earlier in the book, your average retiree would have a large allotment of bonds in her portfolio. The idea was that bonds offered predictable, regular income that would help a retiree sleep well at night. In today's desert of micro interest rates, large pharmaceutical companies, or Big Pharma, offer the next best thing to the security of bonds. Big Pharma pumps out generous dividends with machine-like regularity, while also offering growth that Grandma never could have achieved with bonds.

Many big name corporations have come and gone over the decades. Remember Montgomery Ward? RadioShack? In contrast, America's pharmaceutical giants have remained evergreen. Johnson & Johnson was founded by... you guessed it, the Johnson brothers, all the way back in 1885. In Indiana, they grow both corn and pharmaceuticals. Eli Lilly was founded all the way back in 1876. But all of these youngsters pale in comparison to the granddaddy of them all... Pfizer. If you can believe it, Pfizer was founded by two German Immigrants in 1849. 1849! When Pfizer was founded, owning slaves was legal, there was no such thing as a camera, and electricity hadn't been invented.

Needless to say, investors in Pfizer, Eli Lilly, and J&J have enjoyed generations of prosperity while poor Sears shareholders have been passing through the nine levels of hell. In fact, had you invested $1,000 in Johnson & Johnson in 1977, the year of my birth, today you would have a mind boggling $85,999. The company went public in 1944, and, somewhere out there,

there are families who have been reaping outsized benefits for more than 70 years.

Innovate or Die

So, America's pharmaceutical titans have somehow stayed forever young while corporate giants in other sectors have not stood the test of time. What is the magic trick?

I believe that the trick to achieving solid longevity in the business world is to feel your own mortality every day. Big Pharma draws strength from its smash hits; world beaters such as Prozac, Lipitor, and Viagra come to mind. But each billion-dollar baby is born to die; due to our very well established legal system related to patents, every high ranking pharma exec understands explicitly that no one pill or potion will last forever.

Big Pharma is notorious for employing every legal and semi-legal method for extending medical patents, and wringing every last penny from blockbuster drugs. However, behind closed doors, executive teams know, down to the month, exactly when their golden goose will stop laying eggs.

You could call this "innovate or die." This is the genius of our American creative machine. As much as the scoundrels running Big Pharma would love to ride one or two big products forever, they just can't. Due to the laws of our land, Big Pharma has an unquenchable thirst for new products and new technologies.

Let's contrast Big Pharma's situation with the more typical scenario in other sectors of the economy. There are too many sad stories to count. The pattern is typically that a Fortune 500 company has a huge hit product on its hands, that reliably prints cash year after year, and perhaps even decade after decade. On some level, they know that the party can't last forever, but they don't know it in their bones. Who wants to be the vice president who greenlights big corporate spending on R&D when that very same R&D threatens to replace the company's existing cash cow? For example, did you know that Kodak engineers actually invented the digital camera?

> *"It's no exaggeration to say Kodak invented digital photography. In 1975 Kodak engineer Steve Sasson created the first digital camera, which took photos with 10,000 pixels, or 0.01 megapixels — about a hundredth of the resolution that low-end camera phones have today. Kodak didn't stop there; it worked extensively on digital, patenting numerous technologies, many of which are built into the digital cameras of today......"If you want to point back to the most pivotal moment that caused this," says Hayzlett, "it was back in 1975 when they discovered the digital camera and put it back into a closet......In 1995 the company brought its first digital camera to market, the DC40. This was years before many others would get into the digital game, but Kodak never took advantage of its early start. Philosophically, the company was steeped in the film business, and to embrace digital meant cannibalizing its own business. "It's a classic business strategy problem," says Miriam Leuchter, editor of Popular Photography. "Their whole business was tied up in film and in printing. So while they're developing this business technology, there's not a big incentive to push it very far." (Mashable.com, Pete Pachael, 1/20/12)*

This same sad story has been repeated hundreds of times across the Fortune 500. On the most basic level, major corporations are filled with people who don't fully control their own businesses, and who aren't big risk takers anyhow. That's why they work for a Fortune 500 company. Big Pharma certainly doesn't like risk. But they have no choice.

Even in the glory days of Viagra, when Pfizer was swimming in cash, they knew that Viagra would one day go generic. They could predict Viagra's death down to the month. If anyone was about to bumble into any good new innovations in the lab, shoving that nascent innovation into a closet would be the last thing Pfizer would want. Of course there are no guarantees in life. But so far, Pfizer has outlasted many nations, so the steady cash flow should help a retiree sleep well at night.

Getting The Right Rx

How do you know which Big Pharma stocks are the right ones? Well, the simple answer is that they are almost all the right ones. As we discovered above, most of the big household brands that you know were founded before your grandfather was born. They were good investments for your grandpappy, and they'll be good investments for you.

That being said, a few words of caution. First, not all pharmaceutical stocks are Big Pharma stocks. The world of pharmaceutical investing is roughly divided between Big Pharma and biotech. While both of these groups are dedicated to the discovery and commercialization of new medicines, they are very different kinds of companies with different investor groups.

The world of biotech is for swashbuckling investors who want maximum share price growth. These are typically young, high risk companies that pay no dividend. In fact, many have little if any cash flow at all!

Big Pharma companies are very large, multinational firms that take a more "slow but steady" approach to winning in business. Many medicines start life in the laboratory of an upstart biotech innovator, but wind up being marketed, distributed, and sold by a Big Pharma concern.

The world of biotech is an exciting place for an investor who wants to see his money grow as fast as possible. It's so exciting that I wrote a separate book on that topic (*Your First Biotech Million: How to Earn Your Fortune in Biotech Stocks*). However, if you want to live off dividend income for an indefinite period of time, what you want is a proven, long established business that functions like an ATM machine. That would be Big Pharma.

How do you know which companies are Big Pharma, and which are biotechs? There are a few where the line gets blurry. For example, Amgen and Gilead are often referred to as biotechs because twenty years ago, they were scrappy upstarts. Today, they are behemoths that churn out dividends. Yesterday's biotechs are often today's Big Pharma firms.

According to Becker's Hospital Review, here are the largest global pharmaceutical firms:

The top 10 pharmaceutical companies, ranked by revenue:

1. Pfizer — $51.75 billion

2. Roche — $50 billion

3. Novartis — $47.45 billion

4. Merck — $46.84 billion

5. GlaxoSmithKline — $43.54 billion

6. Johnson & Johnson — $42.1 billion

7. AbbVie — $33.27 billion

8. Sanofi — $27.77 billion

9. Bristol-Myers Squibb — $26.15 billion

10. AstraZeneca — $23.57 billion

Of these, five are based in Europe (Roche, Novartis, GSK, Sanofi, AstraZeneca). The ten pay between 2 and 6% dividends, and those dividends have grown between 5 and 10% each and every year for decades. This means that almost any pharmaceutical stock has grown its dividends at three to four times the rate of inflation. Most of these ten have a total return in excess of 200% over the last decade. Novartis, the laggard of the bunch, has still returned 143%. Good medicine indeed!

Big Pharma is a great business. But it's not the only great business. In the next chapter, we will explore another appealing option.

Chapter 7: Energy Stocks - Powering Your Retirement

Here is a confession for you. I know very little about how the modern world works. When you press the ignition button on your car, why does it start reliably? When you flick your light switch, why do the bulbs suddenly illuminate? I have a very rough idea based on 6th grade science, but if you really pressed me, I would have to admit that it's all black magic to me. The black magic behind modern power generation, distribution, and consumption isn't so important to us as investors. What is more important is how we turn that black magic into green magic; however energy works, it typically works great for dividend investors. Big energy companies have reliably churned out dividends for decades, just as the sun rises and sets with predictable regularity.

An amazing aspect of the energy sector is that, no matter what the inputs, the outputs remain just about the same. That is why I use the term "energy" rather than "oil," "gas" or "wind." It turns out, the more things change, the more they stay the same from the point of view of the income investor. Oil, gas, wind, are all different inputs that lead to the same output; energy that millions of consumers can summon on demand. The science and politics are different depending on how energy is being harnessed, but the underlying business isn't so different. Energy is needed around the globe on a constant and predictable basis; that constant, predictable cash flow lends itself to the sowing and reaping of dividends.

You can literally earn money for yourself every time you start your car or turn on your home oven. Whether you prefer "old school" hydrocarbons or "new school" renewables, this sector produces generous dividends that can power your lifestyle for decades to come.

Black Gold

The most traditional place to look for dividends is in oil stocks. Oil "supermajors" like ExxonMobil and Chevron have pumped out reliable cash flow for decades. According to Dividend.com, in the thirty-year period between 1990 and 2020, Exxon has grown its dividend by roughly 700%. In other words, a yearly payout of $0.48 per share in 1990 became $3.37 in 2020. These kinds of cash flow bonanzas have not been unusual; British Petroleum (BP) grew it's dividend from $0.05 per share per quarter in 1998 to $0.63 per share per quarter just before the coronavirus hit. So, a BP shareholder who had simply bought the stock and then done nothing for 22 years would have seen her annual cash flow grow by 1,260%. By the way, this is during a time period in which BP caused the greatest environmental disaster in history and paid record fines into the multi billions. (The DeepWater Horizon).

Bottom line? Nothing could slake the world's thirst for oil over the last hundred years. Almost any large oil company would have been a great investment for a retiree who wanted to live off of the income.

But is it still a good investment? You may have noticed, the world is starting to change. As I write this, Tesla, an electric car company, has seen its stock surpass every other car manufacturer combined. The United Kingdom has pledged to stop selling internal combustion cars altogether by 2030. More and more people feel that the pollution and geopolitical turmoil that oil causes makes it an unethical industry.

The answer to this question is that oil supermajor stocks remain great investments for the right kind of investors. These stocks are not for everyone. Ironically, there are two specific, opposite groups of retirees that might benefit the most. The first group is risk averse, elderly retirees. The second group, paradoxically, are younger, more aggressive investors who are willing to take a risk.

If you are a traditional retiree trying to navigate a world of micro interest rates, you are looking for companies that will provide steady, predictable income for the rest of your life. At 70 or 75 years old, the "rest of your life" may mean twenty years or so. According to Policyadvice.net, in 2020, electric cars only achieved a 2.2% market share of new cars sold. This means that, of all the new cars sold, 98% were still internal combustion engines. Even if many nations ban internal combustion after 2030 (and that's a BIG "if"), that 98% of new cars sold today will remain on the road for many years to come. It seems clear that electric cars are the future, but sometimes the future can be stubbornly slow in coming. In the meantime, our traditional retiree can kick back and enjoy many more years of steady dividends. If you are currently in your 70s, and you suspect that your investing timeline isn't more than twenty years, oil supermajors may be a good source of income for you.

How could the very same stocks appeal to a younger, thrill-seeking investor? Why would a forty year old want to buy stock in oil companies when oil may be gone by the time she reaches traditional retirement age?

Lately, even some of the most established oil companies in the world have publicly and dramatically committed to transforming into "energy" companies. Slowly ramping down investment in hydrocarbon production, while slowly ramping up investment in wind, hydrogen, and biofuel projects. While this seems shocking at first (as the leopard doesn't often change his spots), there is a certain logic to it.

One of the most promising and rapidly growing fields of renewable energy is offshore wind production. This involves installing massive wind turbines in deep water far off shore. Not an easy task, and one that requires a company with deep pockets and substantial ocean-oriented infrastructure. The argument goes that oil companies have a long history of massive projects deep at sea due to their many adventures and misadventures in deep water oil drilling. Installing windmills the size of the Eiffel Tower may actually be considered easy work compared to the great lengths these companies have gone to extract oil buried under miles of ocean and rock hard ocean floor. The same argument applies for hydrogen. Even though hydrogen is in its infancy, the thought is that liquid hydrogen would function much the same way that oil and gas do today, except in a much more sustainable and eco-friendly manner. The oil supermajors know a thing or two about flammable liquids that need to be transported over vast distances.

The potential for transformation is real, but it won't be quick, and it won't be easy. The risks are large. Many mammoth global corporations simply can't overcome their own bureaucracy to enact effective change. Also, many of these companies have made noises about this kind of transformation before, only for the wheels of change to get stuck. Is the commitment real this time? Both BP and Total, two of Europe's largest oil companies, have publicly pledged to become carbon neutral organizations by 2050. This would mean slowly but surely shifting investment away from oil and gas, and truly becoming energy companies rather than oil companies.

In the meantime, oil companies across the globe are being shunned by investors. BP is yielding between 7 and 8%, Total has hovered around 7%. Exxon Mobil, which has been more reluctant to get on the eco train, has yielded as much as 10%! These are examples of where the sector has fallen out of favor, causing share prices to drop. As cash flow has remained roughly the same, these new energy companies are now deeply discounted. This is why they might appeal to a younger investor who is willing to take a gamble. If they do succeed in weaning themselves off oil and moving into renewables in a big way, there is a lot of upside that other investors have ignored. If these ancient lumbering giants are surpassed by more nimble, more youthful competitors, then they will wind up in the dustbin of history, along with Sears, RadioShack, and Kodak.

The New Kids On The Block

Some people just don't want to go near oil and gas stocks. They feel that hydrocarbons pollute the earth, or they simply don't want to get involved in yesterday's energy technology. If you feel this way, no problem! Wall Street has cooked up something tasty for you. I present: The yieldco. If you need a mean green machine to pump out reliable dividends without pumping oil from Mother Earth, a yieldco investment could be for you.

If you ever were to get involved in the oil business, you might hear terms such as "upstream," and "downstream." These terms revolve around the idea that finding oil, starting up an oil field, and operating an established, profitable field are really separate businesses. It turns out that the dynamic is no different when the source of the energy is renewables.

Yieldcos are companies that are related to large developers of renewable assets. These entities contain the mature, established, cash flow positive assets of these development companies. Yieldcos offer predictable, long term cash flow to investors, while allowing the developers of the renewable assets to "recycle" the capital that they initially deployed to develop the project. Every time a large developer of renewable energy projects successfully stabilizes a wind farm, for example, they sell an interest in the future revenues of that wind farm to a yieldco. The developer can then, in turn, use the same capital again and again to build more and more wind farms. As an investor, you get the income for decades to come.

One example of a yieldco is NextEra Energy Partners (NEP). Although the vehicle is technically a partnership, you can buy and sell shares just like anything else on E-Trade or whatever brokerage you use. NEP is the little brother of NextEra Energy (NEE), a utility and one of the largest developers of renewable energy projects in the United States. NextEra started out its corporate life as Florida Power and Light, a sleepy, government-regulated energy utility that mostly used traditional energy sources to provide regulated electricity to millions of Floridians. About ten years ago, the company radically changed course and embarked on an aggressive program to develop renewable assets around the US.

The strategy worked. Over the last decade, NextEra's share price has rocketed from $12 to $84. The stock currently trades at a price to earnings ratio of 44, which would have been impossible when the company was merely another government-regulated utility.

This legendary share growth is certainly appealing to a wide swath of investors. However, it might not appeal to investors who seek dividend income. Currently, NextEra only yields 1.6%, a far cry from the 3-5% it would have yielded when it was just another utility stock. Never one to leave money on the table, NextEra devised a solution: NextEra Energy Partners, a yieldco that will provide less share price growth, but more current yield. In this way, NextEra management can engage and please two different shareholder constituencies, while recycling capital as described above. NextEra Energy Partners yields 2.81% and is just getting started. According to management, a shareholder could expect this dividend yield to grow by 12-15% annually for the foreseeable future. At that rate, you would double your income every five years. How is that for green energy?

According to the US Energy Information Administration, as of 2020, only 11% of American energy is considered to come from renewable sources. But costs associated with solar power and wind are falling dramatically, while battery technology is constantly improving. Many hope that the United States will extract 100% of its energy from renewable sources by 2050. So that would mean that the epoch of the renewable yieldco is just now beginning. If you want a reasonable dividend that grows quickly and is derived from the latest cutting edge technology, look at names such as NextEra Energy Partners (NEP), Brookfield Renewable Partners (BEP), and Atlantic Yield (AY).

Old School Meets New School

If you don't quite know whether you want tried and true, traditional hydrocarbon stocks, or you want to bet on the new technologies of the renewable world, you can always outsource that decision to experts. You can achieve balance and safety by simply investing directly in electric utility companies. These are publicly traded companies that provide energy as a service directly to consumers and businesses across the United States. Although they trade on the stock exchange just like any other security, they often function in a unique business ecosystem. Often, electric utilities enjoy a monopoly over a certain defined geographical territory in exchange for being regulated by an alphabet soup of different governmental entities. The result is a world of investable companies that are conservative by definition and highly scrutinized by the general public, both good things if you are a retired investor seeking reliable yield. In fact, these companies are so reliable that they have been termed "window and orphan" stocks. Meaning that they are good purchases for unsophisticated, vulnerable inventors who just need steady cash flow.

These electric utilities have a mandate to deliver reliable energy to citizens and reliable dividends to shareholders, so a broadly diversified portfolio of energy assets is the safest approach for them. This means that, as a shareholder, you automatically get "the best of both worlds," a mix of reliable traditional energy sources (natural gas, coal, nuclear) and more cutting edge technologies (solar, wind, biomass). As time goes by and technology progresses, most utilities are using less and less dirty coal and more and more clean sunlight. When you buy shares in these utilities, you are hiring a team of seasoned energy professionals to handle this transition for you. These are the ultimate "set it and forget it" stocks.

That being said, not all electric utilities are the same. Some are more aggressive than others in terms of transitioning to 21st century energy. Some actually own natural gas pipelines. Some, like NextEra, both develop new projects around the country, and own a regulated local utility. Some just provide stodgy old day-to-day energy for specific locals. They may have different dividend yields and different dividend growth rates that reflect some of these distinctions. Below is a list of the ten largest (by market capitalization) utilities so that you can shop and compare:

1. NextEra Energy, Inc
2. Duke Energy Corp
3. Southern Co.
4. Dominion Energy Inc.
5. American Electric Power, Inc.
6. Exelon Corp.
7. Sempra Energy
8. Xcel Energy
9. Eversource Energy
10. Public Service Enterprise Group

(Data: Vanguard.com, February 2021)

Whether you choose the high dividends of oil stocks, the high growth of renewable energy yieldcos, or the balanced approach of electric utilities, energy equities can reliably deliver dividends between 2 and 6%, year after year, decade after decade.

But what if there was a way you could earn more? Much more, without incurring much more risk? What if there were reputable, established businesses that could pay you 7%, 9%, or even 11% on your money? Would that have a dramatic effect on how early you could retire, and on your lifestyle in retirement?

Read on to learn all about these enhanced income options.....

Part 2: Special Vehicles

Chapter 8: REITs - Trustworthy Dividends

Have you ever gone for a ride in your car, looked around at the buildings that you pass, and wondered to yourself, "who owns all this?" The gas station where you filled up, the strip center where you dropped your dog off for grooming, the warehouse that you passed on the highway. We each pass thousands and thousands of buildings every year. Who owns all of that? What if I told you, that "who" could be you?

Most people understand on one level or another that real estate can be a great investment. Yet for many people, the world of real estate seems time consuming, risky, and, more than anything else, complicated. It can be all of those things. If you wanted to own a hundred-unit rental building, you would have to line up millions in financing, find some way of managing unruly tenants, and find methods of maintaining the property without breaking the bank. Imagining those kinds of challenges, too many people stay away.

There is an easier way to enjoy the benefits of real estate ownership without all of the hassle and complication of directly owning strip centers and apartment buildings. A Real Estate Investment Trust, or REIT, is a special kind of investment entity expressly crafted to suit the needs of a passive income investor. A REIT is a simplified vehicle for owning real estate; there are dozens upon dozens of different kinds of REITs that specialize in different kinds of real estate. If you want to own apartment buildings, there are REITs that specialize in apartment buildings. If you want to own nursing homes, there are REITs that specialize in nursing homes. These are typically publicly traded companies that you can buy and sell using the same brokerage where you would buy shares of Google or Facebook.

What Is So Special About REITs?

If you go on E-Trade and start researching REITs, on the surface they will look similar to all of the other stocks. And they do trade with the ease of regular stocks. But there are a few key differences that make REITs especially appealing for income investors.

First is corporate structure. Most large corporations that you would purchase through your brokerage are C corporations. C corporations are almost treated like people by the law, so they pay their own taxes. A C corporation pays dividends to you (or buys stock back) with whatever money is left over after taxes. A REIT is a different legal structure than a C corporation. A REIT is considered a "pass through entity." This means that REITs pay no taxes at the corporate level. To be considered a REIT, the entity must pay out 90% of its profit in the form of dividends. Then the individual shareholders are responsible for the taxes. A C corporation, such as Dow Chemical, must pay taxes at the corporate level, but then can pay out, or not pay out, whatever amount of cash the board of directors decides upon. In order to be classified as a REIT by Uncle Sam, the real estate-owning entity is legally required to pay out 90% of profits. This requirement tends to make REITs lean, mean, dividend-paying machines.

This small difference in corporate structure has some big implications for investors. One aspect is that many investors feel that REITs are more transparent in their accounting and reporting structure. If you were around in the 90s, you may remember Enron, a high flying "technology" company that turned out to be a total fraud. In fact, it's one of the largest corporate frauds in history. Because Enron was considered by the market to be a growth stock, no one expected Enron to pay dividends. This means that Enron could easily embellish, and then outright invent, paper profits, because they never needed to pay out cold hard cash. At some point, they realized their accounting was barely scrutinized, because they were playing with all theoretical values anyhow.

The corporate management of large REITs is the exact opposite. They live under a microscope, because their cash payout must be constant and regular. It's easy to invent profits on the accrual system of accounting, but if your business is secretly flailing, it would be almost impossible to churn out the regular dividends that REIT investors demand. It's easy to fake accounting profits; willing cold hard cash flow into existence is a little tougher.

Along those lines, the accounting terms utilized in the REIT world are slightly different from the Generally Accepted Accounting Principles (GAAP) that are the language of the C corporation. I can already picture you banging your head against the wall. More accounting! Different accounting! First he asked me to learn one language, now I need an additional language?

Yes, and no. The accounting vocabulary around REITs is actually easier than GAAP. The actual vocabulary might seem intimidating at first, but with just a little practice, it's easy. The reason for this is the simplified structure of the REIT entity.

You may recall from earlier chapters that in the world of C corporations—big, well-known concerns such as Microsoft or General Motors—a standard financial report consists of three parts, the profit and loss (P&L), the cash flow, and the balance sheet. You may remember that the P&L is a largely theoretical form of accounting that aims to quantify ethereal costs such as stock options and depreciation, while the cash flow sheet accounts for a business operation as if your kid was running a lemonade stand (cash in, cash out, etc). Furthermore, the balance sheet of a typical C corporation can get complicated, because much of the value of today's C corporations is intangible. If you were running a lemonade stand, it would be easy for you to assign a hard value to your inventory of lemons, sugar, and ice. But if you're running a biotechnology firm that has been developing intellectual property for years with no revenue to show (yet), that asset and liability accounting can get tricky.

You might be surprised, but running a multi-billion dollar real estate business is a lot like running a giant lemonade stand. Because your investors are almost exclusively interested in cash flow, the accounting is much more simple. What the investor really wants to know is; how much cash does the operation throw off? What is the market value of the property that the company owns, versus how much mortgage debt is owed against the properties? Accounting concepts in the world of REITs are very tangible and concrete. If you are accounting phobic, REITs may actually suit you better than other forms of income investing.

If you would like to learn about accounting for Real Estate Investment Trusts, here are a few reliable sources with glossaries and in depth explanations:

-REIT.COM
-REITINSTITUTE.COM
-DIVIDEND.COM

You can also find in-depth yet simple explanations of REIT accounting at fool.com and investopedia.com.

Other Benefits of REITs

One big benefit of real estate investment that is often touted is the very light taxation for investors. This has become a polemic theme over the last few years, as it was revealed that a certain real estate mogul turned United States President has barely ever paid taxes over his long and supposedly lucrative career. The fairness of the system is extremely questionable, but as I write this text, real estate investors still pay very low tax. The reason is the difference between theoretical accounting and actual cash flows.

As we discussed before, GAAP accounting factors in theoretical costs and benefits. This is actually the kind of accounting that our tax system works on. In the world of real estate, the biggest theoretical cost is asset depreciation. In theory, a hard asset loses value over time because it decays and needs to be maintained. These theoretical costs, which are often substantial if you buy a twenty-year-old apartment building, are recorded against real revenue, such as rents. This leads to a situation whereby many real estate projects can show an annual accounting loss (or at least minimal profits) when, in reality, cash flow greatly exceeds hard costs. This means cash flow is positive, even if a loss is recorded on the P&L statement.

Of course, there are many variations on this theme, and big, sophisticated investors who directly own hard real estate utilize an endless playbook of tax minimization plays. Most exploit that difference between "real world" cash flow accounting and "theoretical" GAAP accounting. When you own a stock in a REIT, you get many of those same tax benefits, except you get none of the complexity and headaches. As a shareholder, you have a skilled management team in place who does all of the work for you.

REITs file tax reports to the Federal Government on a GAAP basis. However, the amount of cash that flows to you is determined on a real world basis. This often leads to a situation whereby your REIT dividend theoretically represents more than the profit the company made that quarter. In that case, the REIT is theoretically implementing what is termed a "return of capital"" This means that they are theoretically returning some of your own capital to you, thus, that portion of the dividend isn't taxed. This can mean, for example, that if you received $10 in dividends, only $7 are taxed. In reality, all $10 are profits that the company generated. Through magical accounting pixie dust, you just got a huge discount on your taxes.

The term return of capital is something that we will discuss in several chapters in this part of the book. This is a commonly misunderstood phrase, because it means different things in different circumstances. We will discuss each circumstance as we get to it, but suffice it to say, in the context of equity REITs, return of capital is a good thing. It means lower taxes for you.

Another big benefit of REIT investing is that you can get more than just steady cash flow. Many REITs also appreciate in value over time. Remember, when you own a REIT, it's very similar to you and three partners owning a ten-unit apartment building. In the case of the REIT, there are just a lot more partners. The owners of the apartment building hope to reap regular income from the investment, but they also hope the apartment building will be worth more in ten years than it is now. According to Investopedia.com, the average REIT earned a 10.5% return in the twenty-five years between 1984 and 2019. During that same time period, REITs have yielded an average between 4 and 6%.

You may remember the "Rule of 72." This rule states that you can take the number 72, divide it by a rate of growth or dividend payout, and the resulting number will represent the amount of years to double your capital. In this example, your average REIT returns 10.5% annually, of which 5% is dividend and 5.5% is capital appreciation. So, if we take the 72, and we divided it by 5.5, we find that you would still have doubled your money every 13 years, even if you spent your dividends every quarter. All of that without ever fixing a toilet or chasing a deadbeat tenant for rent. Not bad!

Different Strokes For Different Folks

So, if there are dozens of different kinds of REITs, how do you choose the right ones for yourself?

There are a few different methods; you will use a lot of the same skills that were described in earlier chapters. Remember, REITs trade like any other publicly traded stock; the main difference is the underlying corporate structure. So, you would still pick REITs the way you would pick most stocks.

The first method is to focus on a sector that you know a lot about, or want to know about. In my own case, I am very concentrated in healthcare REITs. These are companies like Ventas, Medical Properties Trust, and Welltower that own broad portfolios of healthcare properties including retirement communities, doctors' offices, clinics, and even scientific laboratories. Before I became an author and professional investor, I was an award-winning medical salesperson for two decades. Healthcare is near and dear to my heart, so it was only logical for me to feel comfortable researching and choosing REITs in this field.

You might like hospitality, or rental apartments. There are many REITs that focus just on those fields. If you think about it, you can probably recall a time when you drove by a certain kind of property and said to yourself, "That looks like a goldmine. I wish I owned that." You can. You can own almost any sub niche of real estate by purchasing shares of a REIT.

Another method would be the fallen angel method described earlier in the book. One example of a fallen angel purchase that has worked out very well for me is SABRA Healthcare REIT, Inc. A few years ago, mainstream healthcare REITs decided that they wanted to get out of the nursing home business. They decided that they wanted to own senior living properties that enjoyed revenue from wealthy old people, or private pay, in industry parlance. These are considered "active senior living communities" for healthy elderly folks who only need a little help to get by. Nursing homes are different. Nursing homes are heavily dependent on Medicaid payments and various state aid schemes; they are not built for active senior living. Nursing homes are built for very sick people who are mostly paid for by the government. The thinking was that depending on the vagaries of our quasi socialistic medical system was bad business. In addition, frankly, true nursing homes are seen as dirty and disreputable. A lot of the more mainstream medical REITs didn't want to be linked with the bad feelings associated with nursing homes, and they didn't want to depend on the government for payment.

A few REITs decided that they were happy to do the dirty work. SABRA Healthcare was one of them. I've had a few personal experiences in my life that have convinced me that, as distasteful as they are, nursing homes aren't going away. In fact, with 10,000 Baby Boomers per day turning 65, the need for extensive end-of-life care will only increase. The fact that nursing homes were shunned by the major healthcare REITs meant I could buy Sabra shares with a yield anywhere from 7 to 10% annually. This was almost double the yield of healthcare REITs that focused on more prestigious businesses, like life science laboratories. I have collected that handsome yield, every quarter like clockwork, for years now. Sabra turned out to be a classic "fallen angel. Great properties sold cheap because they were misunderstood.

As I write this text, the COVID crisis has caused many formerly premium REIT names to sell for very cheap. Simon Mall REIT currently yields over 6%, double what it yielded just a few years ago. Many of the hotel REITs can be had for a song. Sifting through REITs that have been damaged by the pandemic is risky business. Many of these properties are cheap for a reason. But there are some diamonds in with the coals if you care to put on your research glasses and carefully survey the wreckage.

You can also go in the opposite direction. Just as certain stocks can be termed high dividend growth companies, so can REITs. Some REITs may offer relatively low yields today, but giant growth prospects. One example of a growth REIT is Alexandria Real Estate equities. This is a REIT that focuses on developing and acquiring highly specialized laboratories in the life science business. Because the life science business tends to be clustered in several crowded, expensive cities, creating and owning these kinds of properties is challenging to say the least. The big REITs in this space don't have much competition. Alexandria currently yields a paltry 2.58%, but they are anticipating decades of double digit growth as the American biotechnology industry grows and grows. Another example of a REIT planning some big growth is Digital Realty Trust. This is a REIT that owns highly customized properties that house data centers. Today, the REIT yields just 3.1%, but management promises years of stellar growth, as society grows to depend more and more on Big Data, with special storage requirements.

Many investors are excited and motivated when they find out that they can choose from thousands of different kinds of REITs. However, some feel overwhelmed. The many choices can feel like a burden; inexperienced real estate investors may fear an unwise purchase. If that is how you feel, you can always just buy an exchange traded fund (ETF) that offers you a broad diversification of REITs. Any major investment firm offers ETFs that will represent a broad range of real estate investments. You get the same yield that you would get from individual investments, but the chance of your investment going to $0 is miniscule. Look on the websites of companies like Vanguard, iShares, and Proshares to find these ETFs. They should each charge an annual fee substantially less than 1% of the total assets.

Ownership of real estate is a tried and true method of generating income in your sleep. With your REIT dividends showing up every quarter, you should sleep well indeed.

Chapter 9: Mortgage REITs - Solid Paper

Let's jump back in our imaginary car for a moment, and go for that imaginary ride. This time we are going to cruise through some residential neighborhoods filled with single family homes. What do you see? Green lawns and children playing? Neatly arranged stacks of bricks with immaculate paint and sturdy roofs? When I look at a residential neighborhood, all I see is dividends. Every time these folks make a mortgage payment, I get a piece of it. That is because I own mortgage REITs, (mREITs). Long story short, the mortgage debt of the average American family is one of my best paying investments. You can also benefit from America's obsession with home ownership.

This chapter is not a repetition of the last chapter. In the last chapter we discussed regular REITs, which are technically referred to as equity REITs. Equity REITs are corporate entities with special rules that own real estate. Traditional equity REITs own the actual bricks and mortar. Mortgage REITs own the debt associated with real estate. Equity REITs own physical assets, whereas mREITs just own piles of paper.

For many people, the lack of physical assets is off putting. Your typical equity REIT pays between 3 and 6% dividends quarterly, while your typical mREIT pays between 8 and 12% dividends monthly. Mortgage REITs are like financial rocket fuel that can help your retirement soar. However, to the novice investor, they feel risky. If the returns are so high, and the assets aren't even tangible, is it really safe to count on these vehicles for steady retirement income?

If history is any guide, mREITs are a lot safer than they seem on the surface. Annaly Capital Management, the largest mREIT that invests in single family mortgages, has paid a steady dividend every month since 1997. This means that the company weathered at least three stock crashes and the mother of all real estate crashes in 2008 and still never skipped a dividend. Annaly's principal rival, AGNC Investment Corp, can say almost the same. They have been paying steady monthly income for twelve consecutive years. In our latest coronavirus crisis, no major mortgage REIT went bankrupt; a few did trim their dividends, but now those dividends are quickly rebounding.

How can a security pay out 10% month after month with so little risk? To understand the risk profile of the mREIT sector, you need to understand how these companies work, and why they exist.

Simply Complex

Did you know that the American system of home ownership is utterly unique in the world? In most countries, there is no such thing as a thirty-year mortgage. Additionally, in many countries, you need a much larger down payment to buy a house. 50% down, up front, is not uncommon. The idea that an average Joe could buy a house with just 20% down, or 10% down, or even 5% down is uniquely American. In fact, it's not just an unusual system. It's an unnatural system.

When I say unnatural, all I mean is that the American homeownership system is the direct result of massive government intervention. No private lender would ever lend $400,000 to a middle class family where both partners have to work to pay the mortgage, and the family is only one job loss away from default. Even if a private lender would make such a risky loan, they certainly wouldn't do it at today's absurdly low interest rates.

The reason why an average American family can get a mortgage, even with just 5% down and a shaky income situation, is because the Federal Government removes the risk for lenders. That's right, in the vast majority of American mortgages, the lender can't lose because the Federal Government has guaranteed the loan. You wouldn't want to lend large amounts of money at low interest rates to barely solvent families if you bore the true risk. But if you could lend the money with virtually no risk, then you might do it.

I say "might," because even with federal guarantees, lending large amounts of money at low rates over long periods of time is not very sexy. Your risk would be low, but so would your reward. It's asking a lot of a bank to tie up billions upon billions of dollars at 4% interest for decades. So our system has evolved into a situation where most banks simply originate loans. Meaning they go through the time and trouble of building a sales, marketing, and mortgage processing machine, but they don't actually hold the loans at those low interest rates. After they originate the loan, they take the fees, and then sell the loan to someone else. This allows the entire mortgage business to become a fee generation machine for big lenders. They collect fat fees, collect a little interest, sell the loan, and then use the same money all over again to repeat the process. Even with no risk, the interest rates still suck; it's the constant fees and the recycling of money that makes mortgage origination a good business. If the originators could not sell the loans they make, the entire system would ground to a halt.

Which is why mortgage REITs have had such a steady track record. Mortgage REITs buy loans from originators. They don't buy the loans directly. They buy what are called Mortgage Backed Securities, or MBS. Each MBS represents hundreds or thousands of loans that were originated by banks, then packaged and sold to investors as bonds. Mortgage REITs are some of the largest buyers of MBS in the United States. These MBS are fully guaranteed by the Federal Government. The largest, most brand name Mortgage REITs focus on buying Mortgage Backed Securities that are explicitly guaranteed by the Federal Government. The magic of the mortgage REIT is that, when you are the largest buyer of government backed securities, you also have the implicit backing of the Federal Government. Remember, the entire Frankenstein's Monster of a system only works if someone keeps buying the Mortgage Backed Securities that originators create.

Banks and other large lenders originate loans and then sell them, because the characteristics of the loans aren't too sexy. So how can mREITs take a lame 3% interest 30-year loan and transform it into an attractive 10% monthly yield?

The magic that turns lead into gold is leverage. Mortgage REITs borrow money on a short term basis at very low interest and invest that money on a long term basis in the form of mortgage backed securities. The difference between the interest they receive on the mortgage backed securities and the interest they must pay on the short term borrowings is called the Net Interest Margin.

The fact that mortgage backed securities are explicitly backed by the Federal Government means that they are great collateral. You can borrow heavily against them. mREITs use large amounts of leverage, and that is how they wind up squeezing so much juice from a rather unappetizing fruit.

While mREITs are a crucial pillar of American housing, there is still some risk for an investor. The main risk comes in the form of interest rates. The amount of money that an mREIT makes is dependent on that net interest margin, or the difference between long-term and short-term interest rates. The movement of interest rates can be arcane, and at times hard to predict. That is why mREITs are less common than fast food or drycleaning businesses. However, an experienced management team does have a large toolkit to manage these interest rate risks.

Be aware, not all mortgages are guaranteed by the Federal Government, and not all mREITs exclusively buy loans guaranteed by the feds. There are a few extra risky mREITs that specialize in non-guaranteed loans. These are called non agency REITs. But most of the largest names in the business focus exclusively on the conforming FHA loans; the bread and butter of middle class housing. REITs that exclusively buy mortgages backed by the Federal Government are referred to as agency REITs. If you are a conservative investor, I would stick to large, long-established agency REITs such as Annaly Capital, AGNC, or an exchange traded fund that specializes in mortgage REITs, such as iSHARES Mortgage REIT Real Estate fund (REM) or VanEck Vectors REIT Income ETF (MORT).

Never Fear, mREIT Is Here

For the longest time, I couldn't get over the fact that a mortgage REIT was just a pile of paper. It just didn't feel solid to me. But history tells us something different.

If you lived through the Great Recession, you know that it seemed like the entire house of cards was about to tumble down. There had been all kinds of excesses related to mortgage backed securities. It seemed like everyone was getting foreclosed upon, and American housing would never be the same. Everyone said that there had to be reforms; surely big changes were in the works.

That prognostication turned out to be totally incorrect. Twelve years after the real estate crisis to end all real estate crises, what has changed is… nothing. Well, almost nothing. For a long time after the crisis, it was tougher to get a mortgage. Down payment requirements increased. Credit score requirements increased. But now it's almost like the whole thing never happened. I recently had a friend who bought a house with just 5% down. I even know people who went into foreclosure in 2009 who have now bought houses all over again, once again with just 5 or 10% down.

During the worst of the mortgage crisis, few mREITs went bankrupt. In fact, most never even stopped paying a dividend. The fundamentals of our housing system today remain unchanged from 2008. And mortgage REITs are a critical element of those fundamentals. Without the liquidity created by mREITs, millions of middle class people would be unable to own a home. The Federal Government has demonstrated an absolutely ruthless resolve to keep the home ownership contraption alive, even if it remains dependent on government life support. When you bet on a mortgage REIT, you are betting that American society will continue to prize homeownership, and that politicians will do just about anything to keep voters happy.

mREITs have transformed my financial plan. They pay a steady dividend every month, allowing me to plan my life around my monthly "paycheck." I am not particularly risk averse, so most of my mREITs invest in government-guaranteed mortgages, but I do own a few smaller mREITs that invest in non-conforming loans or more specialized niches.

On average, mortgage REITs yield double what most dividend stocks yield. However, be aware that most of the value of mREITs is in the dividend yield. So, for example, a regular equity REIT may yield 4%, but return a total of 11% with share price appreciation over the years. A mortgage REIT may pay out 10% every month, but the share price may not increase much. So, even though the equity REIT pays out less, it may offer larger total returns over the long run. Thus, a well diversified portfolio of income producing equities remains recommendable.

The math and the concepts behind mortgage REITs may seem complicated at first. If you choose to study the industry, you will learn your way, just like any other business. But you only need a simple understanding in order to dramatically increase the yield on your equity portfolio, and dramatically decrease how much you need saved for retirement.

mREITs invest in mortgage debt, and American society is highly dependent upon these entities to continue the tradition of homeownership. mREITs pay monthly, and the payouts can vary depending on trends in interest rates. With that little bit of information, you can increase your monthly income a lot.

Chapter 10: BDCs - Small Loans, Big Dividends

Once you have become comfortable navigating the world of mortgage REITs, your next logical step is to learn about business development companies (BDCs). BDCs are a cousin of the mortgage REIT, both in corporate structure and business concept. If you can understand one, you can understand the other. Business development companies are somewhat more risky than mortgage REITs, but they offer stellar monthly cash flow. A few select BDCs can go a long way toward providing durable income diversification to fuel your retirement.

Much like a REIT, a BDC is a special corporate structure, authorized by Congress, that pays out 90% of its profits in the form of dividends. This means that, much like mREITs, the primary function of the entity is to kick off the maximum cash flow on a regular basis. Investors are only taxed once, at the personal level. It also means that, despite the complicated sounding jargon, the accounting is actually quite easy to understand. The cash flow sheet is what matters by far the most, so the vagaries of the profit and loss statement are less important.

BDCs are also like mREITs in the basic mechanism used to generate cash flow. Business development companies borrow money at very low interest rates and for short time periods, and they invest that money at very high interest rates for longer periods of time. In this case, however, they don't buy mortgages. Business development companies make high interest rate loans to specialized businesses. The result for investors can be monthly income that can equal 10, 11 or even 12% of their total investment.

Why and How

When I first learned about BDCs, my first question was, "why do these entities even exist?" If I wanted a loan for my business, why wouldn't I just go to a bank? Why do BDCs exist when established, big name banks also give out loans?

The answer is related to risk, reward, and regulation. Most banks use the funds of depositors to make loans. This means the hard earned savings of grandmas and average working stiffs. These regular folks deposit their savings with a bank because they believe the savings are safe. This means that banks, by law, have very strict guidelines about how and when they are allowed to utilize depositors money to make loans. Banks are interested in low-risk, low-reward, long-term loans in businesses that are easy to understand.

These restrictions mean that there is a whole world of mid-market firms that would have trouble securing a loan from a bank. An example of a mid-market firm would be a family dry cleaner that had, over time, grown to a chain of one hundred dry cleaners. Or a firm owned by private equity investors that has hundreds of millions of dollars in revenue, but is not generally known on Wall Street or by the general public. For every big name, publicly traded firm like Apple out there, there are tens of thousands of mid-market firms; businesses that are growing rapidly, but not necessarily on any bankers short list of desirable credits.

In particular, BDCs tend to thrive by servicing niche markets. One example of a niche BDC that does very nicely is Horizon Technology Financial Corporation (HRZN). Horizon specializes in loans to mid-market companies in the biotech and IT sectors. Horizon makes secured loans, which can utilize intellectual property as collateral for a loan. Can you imagine your average loan officer at Bank of America trying to figure out the collateral value of a new molecule? This is why dozens of companies have turned to Horizon. They need a lender that understands their particular niche.

A lot of BDCs specialize in short-term, high-interest rate loans. One could use the term bridge loan. An example would be a biotech that is planning to go public in the next year. The time between the company filing its paperwork to go public and the day of the actual IPO could be 12 months or more. This would mean that the biotech is expecting a big influx of cash soon. In fact, they may actually be working with an underwriter on the IPO that has guaranteed a big influx of cash. But in the meantime, the biotech may actually need more cash to ramp up operations in expectation of this IPO. They wouldn't want to sell stock, because they have this big liquidity event coming up, and they don't want to dilute the ownership stake of the existing shareholders. Enter the BDC. The BDC provides a high interest loan, secured against intellectual property, that only lasts for a year. When the biotech client goes public, they immediately turn around and pay off the high interest loan. Meanwhile, the BDC has made great interest, and can now turn around and recycle the same money. If you repeat this same process while minimizing any loan losses, the situation gets lucrative very quickly. That high rate of income and the recycling of capital is why many BDCs can pay an investor double-digit dividend yields month after month.

Risks

So, BDCs share a lot of factors in common with mortgage REITs. One thing that BDCs do not share in common with agency mortgage REITs is that they are not investing in loans that are guaranteed. Which means BDC management teams are borrowing money to turn around and lend that money to smallish corporations that can default. In theory, this makes BDCs risky. But many BDCs have done a thorough job of managing risk.

If you want to see an example of how a sharp BDC management team can navigate risky waters, check out New Mountain Financial Corporation (NMFC). New Mountain focuses on what they call defensive sectors, i.e. business sectors that are resistant to economic downturns. This theory was put to a radical test during the worst of the coronavirus crisis. With America closing down, and businesses failing left and right, these were scary times for business development companies.

NMFC responded by providing extensive transparency to investors. They furnished frequent reports quantifying and explaining the financial situations of each of the loans that they had outstanding. They made some swift moves to limit their exposure to the worst hit sectors of the economy, and maximize exposure to sectors that "won" the coronavirus crisis.

The result? Not only did NMFC not go bankrupt during this time of national crisis, but investors would have barely noticed any crisis at all if they hadn't been paying careful attention. The company did temporarily trim their dividend by less than 20%. But other than that, the cash flow kept rolling, month after month.

Not every BDC did this well, but a surprising number of lending corporations came through the entire ordeal unscathed. This means that BDCs have earned a place in the income portfolio of any investor who lives off of passive income.

How To Invest

There are dozens of different business development companies out there. Not all are created equal. How do you choose the right ones for your portfolio?

One approach is simply to go with the largest companies. Larger companies have deeper pockets, better connections on Wall Street, and larger stakeholders that make it hard for them to go bankrupt. According to theblalance.com, here are the ten largest business development companies by assets under management as of Spring 2021.

1. Ares Capital Corp (ARCC): $6.96 billion
2. Owl Rock Capital (ORCC): $5.70 billion
3. Prospect Capital Corporation (PSEC): $3.20 billion
4. FS KKR Capital Corp (FSK): $3.03 billion
5. Golub Capital BDC, Inc (GBDC): $2.35 billion
6. Goldman Sachs BDC Inc (GSBD): $1.57 billion
7. Main Street Capital Corp (MAIN): $1.43 billion
8. New Mountain Finance Corp (NMFC): $1.19 billion
9. Hercules Capital (HTGC): $1.18 billion
10. TPG Specialty Lending Inc. (TSLX): $1.14 billion

If you stick with the top half of this list, you gain a degree of safety due to sheer size.

Another way of selecting some good BDCs for your income portfolio is to choose companies that specialize in a niche that you know. For example, I know a lot about biotech (I actually wrote a book on the subject, Your First Biotech Million). That is why I chose Horizon Technology (HRZN). They make loans to a lot of biotech concerns. I feel that I am in a unique position to understand the quarterly reports they send me, and take action if necessary. (That would be rare, by the way. I almost always buy and hold).

There are dozens of BDCs that serve specialized niches. If you feel that you know a lot about construction, you can find a fund that specializes in construction lending. If you feel that you know a lot about IT, you can find a firm that focuses on information technology. Everybody knows about something. Leverage your knowledge to pick some winners.

Lastly, if you just want a taste of the sector, but don't want to spend time and energy researching something that is not your core competency, you can always buy an exchange traded fund that represents the sector. This way, you will gain broad exposure to the asset class, without betting too much on any one sector. Because the BDC sector is itself considered to be a niche investment, one of the few pure play ETFs is BIZD (Van Eck Vectors ETF BDC INCOME ETF). This exchange traded fund is currently paying a meaty 9.4% yield, delivered to your inbox monthly. Many other alternative income exchange traded funds offer some amount of BDC exposure. One example would be the Global X Superdividend Alternative ETF (ALTY). Although this exchange traded fund does not focus purely on BDCs, it offers a broad range of high dividend, niche companies that favor big cash flow. ALTY pays slightly north of 8% dividend yield at the moment.

If you think of your retirement income portfolio as a savory gumbo, with many tasty ingredients all boiling together in a pot, you can consider the BDC sector as a dash of cayenne pepper to give the gumbo some kick. You would never want your portfolio to have more than 5 or 10% exposure to business development companies. But just a dash of these high dividend yield corporations can spice up your retirement income in a flash.

Chapter 11: Preferred Stocks - For Those Who Prefer Safe Income

One of the big reasons why I wrote this book was because traditional retirement planning has changed radically in just a few short years. I wanted to help people navigate those changes. You'll remember the big change that we discussed earlier is that bonds, the cornerstone of retirement income for most of the 20th century, have been rendered all but useless due to ultra low interest rates.

Why exactly is it that bonds were so popular to begin with? In the world of finance, where complicated events often have complicated explanations, this explanation is easy. It boils down to just one word. Safety. Bonds were very popular for decades on end because they were an extremely safe investment for retirees who just wanted modest, regular income to pay their rent.

The Federal Reserve has all but taken away that option for most retirees. Today, most decent bonds pay 3% interest or less. Many bonds have had protective covenants reduced or removed entirely so they are no longer the safe harbor they once were.

With inflation taken into account, most bond investors lose money every quarter. But, as the saying goes, "where there is a will, there is a way." If you long for bond-like safety, but need decent income, there is still a way that you can achieve this goal. Preferred stocks are a separate class of securities that offer the best of both worlds: the security of a bond with the beneficial tax treatment of a stock. Even in this era of micro interest rates, preferred stocks may be a great answer for investors who prefer safe income.

Half and Half

Preferred stocks are often referred to as hybrid securities. They offer a mix of bond-like and stock-like features. Sort of the financial equivalent of a platypus. The different features, grafted together, may seem unnatural at first, but this odd mix has actually survived for a very long time, and fends for itself quite nicely in the financial jungle.

Preferred stocks have existed as a class of securities for many decades. There are some records of preferred shares existing even hundreds of years ago. Simply put, preferred shares are a kind of stock that prioritizes income over appreciation and control. Many of the world's biggest, best-known companies offer preferred shares; they offer more income and more safety for your average investor, even if they offer less total upside than common shares.

First, let's talk about safety. When a company goes bankrupt, the courts may decide to liquidate the company's assets. In these cases, bond holders and other debt holders get first right of repayment from the liquidated assets of the deceased company. If there are any assets left after that debt repayment, then preferred shareholders get repaid. Common shareholders always come last in a bankruptcy; they typically get nothing. So, while preferred shares are less safe than bonds, they are still more safe than common stock. And remember, many of the world's largest, most established companies offer preferred shares, so bankruptcy is unlikely to begin with.

Preferred shares also offer a more secure and regular stream of income for shareholders. Although most large, established companies prioritize paying a regular dividend every quarter, they don't have to. Each quarter, the board of directors reviews financial results, and decides how much dividend to pay based on a wide variety of factors. In times of trouble, a dividend can be slashed or eliminated altogether. Not so with preferred shares.

Preferred shares are sold with a pre-determined, fixed rate of yield, that must be paid every quarter. So, while the board can slash a common stock dividend for any reason, at any time, the preferred shareholders must be paid a fixed amount. If the company hits desperate times and is teetering on bankruptcy, the board of directors may halt the dividend for everyone. But this is only in the most extreme and rare situations. Many preferred shares offer a feature known as cumulative dividends. This means that, if an emergency occurs and the board suspends dividends for everyone, then a debt accrues to the company, and all preferred shareholders must be paid back dividends before common shareholders get a penny. These features wind up delivering a high level of safety to income dependent investors.

Preferred shares typically yield about double what common stocks pay. As I write this, the average S&P 500 stock pays just over 2% dividend yield. Many of those very same mega corporations also offer preferred shares that pay 4 or 5%.

It should be noted that although preferreds are often called hybrid securities, they still qualify as stock in the eyes of your Uncle Sam. This means that they receive a beneficial level of taxation next to bonds. Details can vary based on your particular tax bracket and situation, but many investors would pay much lower taxes on income derived from preferred shares as opposed to bonds. Consult with your CPA.

Of course, nothing in life is free. In exchange for great income and superior safety, investors in preferred shares give up a few things. First, preferred shares do not have voting rights. So, a preferred investor has the best claim on a corporation's income, but no claim on governance when proxy vote time comes. Second, a preferred shareholder will rarely see price appreciation on her shares the way a common shareholder might. Preferred share prices are more likely to be governed by fluctuations in interest rates than the supply and demand dynamics that govern common share pricing. A lot of retirees have enjoyed steady, soothing income from preferred shares, but few have gotten rich this way.

Risks

While preferred shares are low risk investments, they are not risk free. Like any investment, there are a few risks that an investor should understand. In this case, there are some unique risks that relate to the hybrid structure of the securities.

The two biggest risks have to do with interest rates. If rates are rising, this may hurt the market value of your preferred shares. For example, let's say that you purchase some preferred shares in Bank of America today at 5% yield. Right now, that is an amazing yield at fairly low risk, because a ten-year treasury bond, the gold standard of credit quality, yields something in the range of 1%. But let's say interest rates rise dramatically over the next five years. Now you can buy a ten-year treasury bond for 4%. That would hurt the market value of your preferred shares. That is because risk averse investors will now flock to the treasury bonds. The closer the treasury yield gets to the yield on your preferred shares, the less valuable your preferred shares may be. The scenario I am describing here hasn't happened in decades, because rates have only moved in one way (down) for a long, long time. However, if rates were to rise substantially, you could get hurt.

It's important to note that in the "bad" scenario above, nothing about your income even changes. If you are happily living your retired life, and you use the steady income from your preferred shares to pay for your lifestyle, you may not even care if the market price of the security goes down. The cash flow coming from the shares stays the same. But it is a risk you should be aware of.

The other big risk also has to do with interest rates, but it's actually the opposite of the prior scenario. If you own a preferred security at 5%, and market interest rates fall precipitously, the issuing company may have the right to call the shares. This means that they can redeem the shares at their par value, without any regard to what you actually paid for the shares. They would do this because, now that interest rates have fallen, they can redeem your 5% shares and offer new 4% shares to the public. Since prevailing interest rates have fallen, they can pay less yield and still be competitive.

Calls have happened a lot over the last few decades, as interest rates have fallen and fallen. There was a time when many preferred shares paid 10% yield! Obviously, those have mostly been called and replaced with lower yielding securities. This phenomena can be damaging for a retiree. If you are happily receiving 5% yield, and your shares get called, then you may have to replace those old shares with new, lower yielding shares. That can hurt your cash flow on a practical level. The good news is that, as I write this text, interest rates are at an absolute rock bottom. They have fallen so far, for so long, that calls now seem unlikely. If interest rates rise from 2021 levels (a huge "if") then this risk may be something you need to factor in.

The last risk is simple liquidation risk. Although bankruptcies are rare with major corporations, it does occasionally happen. If you were a bond holder of Lehman Brothers when they went bankrupt back in 2009, you did better than if you were a holder of preferred shares. (Remember, debt holders are first in the repayment line, preferred shareholders are next). This is why you shouldn't just buy any preferred share from any company without investigating. Do your research, buy names you know, and scour the media landscape to make sure that you avoid media red flags on any particular company.

Looking For Safety

You can buy preferred shares through whatever stock brokerage you typically use. If you opt to own individual preferred shares, the biggest issuers are often banks and utilities. You can often buy from big names such as Bank of America, Citibank, Duke Energy, or NextEra Energy. The fact that these titans of business are household names means that you can easily find research reports on the companies and you can easily access their financial statements to make your own assessment of their financial strength.

Another great way to go with preferred shares is to buy the preferred shares of equity REITs and mortgage REITs. A lot of investors feel that this is a very safe investment, for the following reason: REITs only exist to pay dividends. They are specifically set up as cash flow machines, with stock appreciation a distant second priority. This means that the management is very, very unlikely to cut the dividend of a REIT. As a counter example, Disney recently cut their dividend simply because management thought they could invest that money in building up their streaming service, and the market value of the shares would rise. Disney management is more focused on share price and less on the dividend. REIT managers are famous for obsessing over the cash flow necessary to grow the dividend; they know that the dividend is what keeps their shareholders around. Thus, preferred shares offered by real estate companies are often considered among the safest.

Another way to manage your risk is to simply buy exchange traded funds that represent a basket of preferred shares. This move may not eliminate your interest rate risk, but it brings the risk of bankruptcy almost down to zero. One company can go bankrupt, bringing your investment down to zero. A basket of fifty companies, many of which are big, well known banks and utilities, is very unlikely to lose all of your investment. The Invesco Preferred fund (PGX) and the Global X Preferred ETF (PFFD) are two great options that pump out steady, tax-favored dividends, quarter after quarter, year after year.

Sadly, no one can wave a magic wand to bring back the days when ultra safe bonds paid 5, 6, or 7% per year. But preferred stocks can still fill that fixed income gap in your portfolio. Remember the platypus; it may display a weird mix of features for a living creature, but apparently the design works. The animal has thrived for long periods of time. So have preferred stocks.

Chapter 12: Closed End Funds - Open the Door to Income

You may have noticed by now that as we have moved through part II of this book, we have spent a lot of time discussing interest rates and the borrowing of money. That is because our current ultra low interest rate environment is a classic double-edged sword. On one hand, the only reason why this book is necessary at all is because interest rates are so low that a retiree would struggle to live off the interest from traditional investments. But on the other hand, interest rates are so microscopic that now is a great time to borrow money. As you may remember, both mortgage REITs and business development companies exist almost exclusively because of borrowed money, or leverage in industry parlance.

Does this mean that you should start borrowing lots of money yourself to invest? Probably not (although we will discuss a specific tactic in the next chapter). Borrowing money at any interest rate comes with outsized risks, and is best managed by a team of professionals.

But what if I told you that you can hire such a team of professionals for a modest fee? What if I told you that there is a kind of investment security created specifically to benefit from borrowed money, but at the same time designed to limit your risk?

These securities are known as closed-end funds. Closed end funds (CEFs) are a world unto their own. There are many different kinds, all of which target different investment objectives. But they all have a few things in common. They utilize leverage to create more income than is commonly available on the market. They contain the risks of leverage and leave those risks to professionals. They trade like a regular stock that you can buy and sell on E-Trade, Charles Schwab, or whatever brokerage you use.

On the Highway to Income

You really can visualize a CEF as a financial vehicle. That is because a CEF itself is a kind of entity that carries other securities inside of it. For example, the Tekla World Healthcare Fund (Ticker: THW) is a closed-end fund that carries within it shares of major publicly traded healthcare companies. Also within the fund is a certain amount of borrowed money. This means that the fund yields 8.2% monthly; if you had bought the healthcare shares outright, they might only yield 3% quarterly. In this example, the CEF is the vehicle and the securities and leverage inside are the passengers.

You can think of the CEF world as a highway. At any moment when you are driving down a crowded highway, you might see hundreds of different kinds of vehicles; some large like a bus, others small like a Fiat. Each vehicle might have different passengers. But they all have a few key things in common; they all have wheels, they all have a steering wheel, and they are all trying to get somewhere. Same thing with closed-end funds.

On the highway to income, you might see Tekla World Healthcare, which borrows a lot of money and specializes in brand name healthcare stocks. But you might also see a fund that invests in municipal bonds, a different one that carries utility stocks, and finally a third one loaded with preferred shares. Each one may carry different quantities of borrowed money, and each one may have a management (or driver) who drives more or less aggressively. But almost everything on this highway pays better dividends than regular stocks.

Why are these vehicles called closed-end funds? What does that even mean? Well, an open-end fund is a typical mutual fund or exchange traded fund, where the fund's managers can create just as many shares as the market demands. So the share price of the mutual fund or exchange traded fund typically very closely tracks the value of the underlying assets (also known as NAV, net asset value). In a closed end fund, the entity only has so many fixed shares. So the shares themselves trade based on supply and demand, and may exceed the NAV in value, or lag the NAV. This can create mismatches that can be exploited by astute investors. It's not uncommon for a closed end fund to trade below the value of the fund's assets. So, a closed end fund consisting of utility stocks could trade at $10 per share on the open market, but the NAV is currently $11. In this case, you can buy shares in the fund for less than the current value of the underlying assets. As you might guess, this is called buying at a discount. You could literally get a $1 worth of value for $0.90!

Typically, open-ended mutual funds and exchange traded funds don't employ leverage. So, whatever yield the underlying securities produce is what you get. For example, the Select Spider Healthcare ETF (Ticker: XLV), one of the most widely held open-ended healthcare funds, currently yields about 1.6%. The Tekla World Healthcare fund pays around 8% every month! Leverage is the magic fuel that has turbo charged the Tekla vehicle. That sucker is now flying down the highway.

Some Words About Leverage

If leverage can boost your dividends from 1.6% to 8%, it must be the greatest thing ever, right? Does that mean that everyone should be borrowing?

No. There are a few times when I might recommend that regular investors borrow at today's crazy low interest rates, but generally it's too risky for most people.

Investing borrowed money is the only way that you can actually lose more than you own. If you have $100 to invest, and you make a poorly advised bet, you can lose all of the $100 (although this is very rare). Then you have $0. That outcome hurts, but may not be the end of the world.

If you have $100 to invest, and you borrow another $100 to invest, then you can potentially lose $200. At the end of this bad bet, you are actually $100 in the hole! Investing with borrowed money is often a "live by the sword, die by the sword" proposition, and typically not suitable for your standard retiree. (There is one big exception that we will discuss in the next chapter).

When you choose to invest in a closed-end fund, there are a few protections that moderate your risk. First and foremost is the law. CEFs can only take on a certain amount of debt as per the law. According to the Investment Company Act of 1940, the maximum amount of debt that a CEF can carry is $1 for every $3 in assets (33.3% of assets). To put things in vehicle terms, this means that each car on the highway must have, at a minimum, a seat belt, good breaks, and a reasonable speed limit.

Another reason why leverage is best left to a CEF is because the sponsors of these companies have deep Wall Street connections and can borrow money on very good terms. At this point, many of the larger CEFs are literally borrowing money at interest rates of less than 1%, with very flexible repayments terms. It's highly unlikely that you, as an individual amateur investor, could borrow money on these fabulous terms.

Lastly, most CEF managers have decades of experience in very specific niches. The fact that the industry is regulated by a law that was promulgated in 1940 demonstrates that these managers potentially bring a lot of experience to the table. They are not necessarily any smarter than you, but they are more experienced. They may know when to hit the gas and when to hit the breaks in terms of leverage, and they may utilize sophisticated derivative strategies (calls and puts) to protect against sudden movements in interest rates. Oftentimes, they also have very deep expertise in the particular securities that their fund invests in. For example, the Double Line Income Solutions Fund (Ticker: DSL) boasts a team of managers that specializes in mortgage bonds and foreign sovereign bonds. They don't do pharma stocks or utility stocks; they just offer dozens of years worth of experience in certain kinds of bonds. Can you say the same for yourself?

Red Light, Yellow Light, Green Light

As you are cruising down the CEF highway, there are some key factors that need to be considered as you select the right funds for you.

The first thing that you need to check when a fund grabs your eye is if the fund can cover its monthly dividend distributions through organic earnings. If a fund meets its monthly obligations through return of capital, that is a yellow or a red light.

You may remember that we used the term return of capital earlier in our discussion of REITs. While in the REIT world, return of capital can be a good thing, in the CEF world, the same term means something very different. Closed-end funds are famous for steady, generous monthly distributions. But it's important for you to understand just a little bit about the engine that makes your vehicle function.

Most CEFs follow what is referred to as a managed dividend policy. This means that every fiscal year, the board of directors decides on a fixed amount of dividend and pays that amount out every month. The idea is to provide certainty and regularity to retirees like yourself who live off those dividends.

There are four ways that a CEF can generate those payments every month. The first way is through net investment income. This means that, in any given month, the securities inside the fund threw off enough cash to meet the monthly distribution goal. Because up to 33% of the securities were purchased with debt, they should throw off more income than a normal portfolio with no leverage would throw off. Strong, consistent net investment income is a big green light for you.

The second way that a fund could generate cash for monthly distribution would be through net realized short-term capital gains. This would mean that the share price of the passenger securities within your vehicle have appreciated lately. So management choses to sell some of those shares, reaping the capital gains, and funnel some of the profits your way. This is a good enough way to generate income for investors, but it's the reason why CEFs don't appreciate over time the way a plain exchange traded fund would. Most of the benefit you will receive as a shareholder in a CEF will come from your monthly income; that is because some or all of the capital gains are liquidated on a regular basis and paid out to you.

The third way that a fund could generate that monthly cash payout would be net realized long-term capital gains." This is exactly the same concept as method number two, except it's selling some passenger securities that have been inside the fund for a long time. The only difference between method #2 and method #3 is taxation. Long-term capital gains are taxed at a lower rate than short-term, so that makes method #3 somewhat preferable.

Your yellow light or red light occurs when you see "return of capital." In this context, this means that your fund did not generate enough money this month to make the payout, so the fund is just taking a portion of your own invested capital and handing it right back to you. This can be a useful and beneficial tool to some fund managers in some cases, but it's often widely abused.

Return of capital is a beneficial tool in some cases because it allows management to maintain the managed distribution policy without disturbing the regularity of your income. So, for example, if a certain fund pays you $100 every month, for years on end, and one month the fund doesn't generate that much cash organically, the fund managers might employ the return of capital. That way, your monthly income is not interrupted, and your lifestyle is not disturbed. They might send you $50 from profits, and $50 from return of capital. Or $90 from profits and $10 from return of capital. Or, on some really bad months, 90% return of capital.

You might remember from our chapter on REITs that in that world, return of capital is merely an accounting term with little relation to reality. In the CEF world, return of capital has real consequences. Whatever amount is sent to you that is not profit, (i.e. return of capital) gets deducted from your fund's net asset value (NAV). In other words, in the CEF world, return of capital literally means return of capital, so the value of the assets of your fund is reduced. If we go back to our vehicle analogy, when a CEF returns your capital, they are throwing things out the window. First they throw out a passenger's sunglasses. Then they throw out a passenger's iPhone. If management isn't careful, they wind up throwing whole passengers out of the vehicle. You left your destination with ten passengers loaded with belongings and arrived at your destination with just seven passengers stripped of their sundry possessions. Not good. Not good at all

Unfortunately, the apparent complexity of this situation scares away too many investors from what is really a superior asset class. If this all sounds too complicated for you, stay calm! I am about to make it very easy.

It's very easy to check on the health of any closed-end fund. Simply look for a document entitled 19(a). "19a" stands for Section 19(a) of the 1940 Investment Company Act. That's right, CEFs have been compelled to follow more or less the same rules of the road for more than 80 years. If millions of Americans have figured these rules out over several generations, you can, too.

You can typically find these 19(a) forms on the website of any closed-end fund. The 19(a) form is a simple form that the fund must file, every month, that explains the source of it's distributions for that month. For example, if you go to the website for the Cohen & Steers Infrastructure Fund (ticker: UTF), you can easily find monthly 19(a) forms going back for years.

This form is a very basic grid that will show you, each month, where your payment came from. If your payment was 90% net investment income and 10% return of capital, the form will show that clearly. And vice versa.

The Cohen & Steers Infrastructure Fund is an example of a CEF that has used return of capital responsibly. After clicking on a few of the 19(a) forms from 2020 and 2019, it's plain to see that most months, their payment comes from net investment income and long-term capital gains. Occasionally, when they have a bad month, they use return of capital to fill in that gap. That way, I can count on my steady payments no matter what. That small amount is deducted from the underlying net asset value. But in good months, they replace what they took out, and in fact, over the last decade, the fund's net asset value grew by about 10% a year, despite the occasional returns of capital. This is a status green light.

Other funds are not as responsible. They over promise on their monthly distributions in a bid to attract as many investors as possible. They know they can abuse return of capital, slowly depleting the NAV, because they are counting on an investor base that is not educated, does not ask questions, and does not supervise management. As long as you check those 19(a) forms a couple times of year, that group of chumps will not include you.

Navigating NAV

The concept of net asset value ("NAV") in regards to CEF share price is also a critical bit of mechanics to understand. A solid understanding of this idea will power your portfolio to profit.

To review, the CEF is the vehicle, and the NAV are the passengers within the vehicle (the assets). Sometimes, the passengers within the vehicle are worth more than the vehicle itself, and sometimes the vehicle fetches more on the open market than the passengers alone would. When the shares of a CEF trade for less than the value of the NAV, then they are said to be trading at a discount. When the CEF shares trade for more than the NAV, then they are trading at a premium. The discrepancies between these two prices can turbo charge your profits.

Sometimes, there is a good reason why shares of a CEF might trade for less than the NAV. Maybe the whole sector is depressed and has attracted negative media attention (2020 was the annus horribilis for oil, for an example). Maybe the fund in particular has problems (accounting scandal, corporate takeover drama, etc). But very often, whole sectors simply fall out of fashion for very little reason. As we've discussed, this is like the Z-Cavarricis lurking in the back of your closet. There is nothing wrong with them; they were fine garments when you originally bought them, and in fact, you could wear them today, if you could stand being mocked by your colleagues. ("Hey, the 90s called, they want their pants back!"). People that enjoy bargain hunting can find some real value in the CEF space by looking to buy funds that are trading at a discount to their NAV.

Let's look at my investment in the Tekla World Healthcare Fund (Ticker: THW). When I bought this fund, it was trading at a discount to NAV of about 10%. The thinking was that Donald Trump was going to take a wrecking ball to the American pharmaceutical industry and that long threatened pricing reforms would greatly limit Big Pharma's profits moving forward. I never believed in that theory, and I'm just a nerd for healthcare stocks, so I bought THW. At the time, the CEF was yielding in the range of 9%. So, for every $1,000 I invested, I could get an annual payout of $90 while I waited for the world to come to its senses on healthcare.

Guess what? They did. Big Pharma weathered the storm of hot air about pricing reform (as they always have) and then COVID-19 happened. All of a sudden, instead of being the boogieman of American capitalism, Big Pharma was viewed as the hero. In America's time of need, they came running for help, and Big Pharma produced massive quantities of highly efficacious vaccines in record time. To return to the fashion analogy, suddenly those Z-Cavarrichis came roaring back into fashion, and you were the first guy at the party to rock that style. After all, you never threw them out to begin with. Today, Tekla World Healthcare Fund actually trades at a premium of about 10% to the NAV. So, not only have I collected a juicy 9% dividend every month for years, I have also enjoyed substantial price appreciation on my shares.

Am I some kind of investing genius? Not really. I just learned the rules of the road and learned to drive astutely. You can do the same.

Vehicle Shopping

Armed with knowledge, you are ready to hit the CEF highway. These funds typically pay between 4 and 10% monthly dividends, often on a tax advantaged basis. These strong, steady payouts can make a huge difference in your retirement income.

As we said earlier, there are thousands of different CEFs with as much variety as that crowded highway we have been talking about. There are few different ways that you can shop.

The first way is to choose a sector and work backwards. In my example, I have a particular interest in healthcare stocks; this led me to Tekla World Healthcare Fund. Maybe you like municipal bonds, or utility stocks, or even preferred shares. All of these are different kinds of passengers that can be stuffed into a CEF vehicle. The reason why you would buy them through a CEF as opposed to an exchange traded fund or directly would be because the CEF will provide higher yield. As stated earlier, Tekla World Healthcare often yields 8% or more, while the underlying stocks, if bought directly, would only yield between 2 and 4%.

Another example would be CEFs that invest in municipal bond funds. My elderly aunt loves to invest in municipal bonds. These are ultra safe bonds issued by state and local governments to pay for municipal projects, such as water and sewer. These bonds have been a staple of retirement planning for decades because they are very safe and offer tax free yield. However, in the last decade or so, "muni bonds," as they are called, have offered less and less yield to the point that you would be lucky to collect 2% on your money. Now my aunt buys muni bonds through closed-end funds and she can collect 4% or more, tax free (note: taxation treatment of CEFs is related to the taxation treatment of the underlying securities. Consult your CPA).

The risk profile of the CEF is somewhat more than if you bought the securities directly. That is because the funds employ leverage. However, much of this risk is simply volatility, meaning that the price of the fund may fluctuate somewhat more than the underlying securities would if held directly. So, when choosing how much of your portfolio to allot to CEFs, be aware that they are somewhat more volatile than lower yielding options. However, the chances of your CEF value going to $0 are very remote. Remember, each CEF has dozens of investments inside of it. It would take a cataclysmic event for that many names to fail all at once.

So, you can shop for closed-end funds by first choosing a sector, then finding funds that cater to that sector. If you are a value shopper, like myself, a different method may appeal to you.

You can run a screen to help you focus only on funds that are currently trading at discount to NAV. This is like going to the Goodwill and hunting for treasure among the trash. If you find ten CEFs where the NAV is worth more than the open market share prices, there will be a reason for eight of those funds. For two out of ten, the shares will just be on sale for no apparent reason. The CEF market is very inefficient, and a determined shopper can find some real deals and steals.

It might seem intimidating at first to sift through hundreds of coals to find a few glittery CEF diamonds. But there is a whole community out there that can help you. Closed-end funds investors are the Trekkies of the investment world. They have a cult-like devotion to their niche, and they often gather online, or sometimes in person, to exchange tips and tricks. People really geek out over closed-end funds ("Set your phasers to 'profit!')

There are dozens of newsletters you can subscribe to where they have done a lot of the research for you in terms of identifying undervalued CEFs. These newsletters can range from $9 per month to $99 per month; a great deal compared to the cost of an MBA. There are also countless analysts on Seeking Alpha who specialize in closed-end funds. For a very modest subscription fee, you can browse a wide variety of CEF research.

You can also just do the research yourself. Like anything else, it seems hard at first, but becomes exceedingly easy with practice. In both of the examples that we have discussed in this chapter (Cohen & Steers and Tekla), all of the information you would ever need is posted directly on their websites. You can compare NAV to share price, you can compare NAV to share price over time, you can check out those all-important 19(a) notifications, and you can read detailed biographies of the fund's management.

When you are working a job for a living, you have no residual. Even though I was an award-winning salesperson, I was only as good as my last sale. I worked, I got results, I got paid. The very next week, it was back to work, hoping to get results, hoping to get paid.

When you teach yourself how to shop for closed-end funds, you only need to do the work one time. It might take you a few months to learn the basics, and a few years to get really good. But once you have learned how to do it, then you know how to do it. You do the research once, you buy the securities once, and then you put up your feet and enjoy the fruit of your hard work for decades to come. Does this sound like a good "job" to you?

Closed-end funds have been popular high yield investments since at least 1940. This is because they use leverage in a controlled, focused way without burdening the investor with the risks that come with directly borrowing money. For most retirees, this indirect borrowing is all the leverage they would ever need. But there are a few cases when it pays to borrow directly. We will conclude the special vehicles section of this book by examining some special scenarios where borrowing directly is the smartest move.

Chapter 13: Borrow Your Income

Here is a quick historical quiz for you. Complete the following aphorism: "The only sure things in life are death and..."

Even if you don't like history, you may very well know the phrase. If you have made some money in business you certainly know the phrase.

"The only sure things in life are death and taxes." - Benjamin Franklin.

No one really likes taxes. They are a necessary part of society, and the law should be followed at all times. But most people are always happy to hear about ways that taxes can be minimized while still following the law. When interest rates are this low, one great way to minimize your taxes is to borrow against your stocks for your spending money. This works especially well with dividend stocks.

Income from stock dividends and stocks sales is categorized as capital gains and often taxed at rates between 0% and 23%. (If you only hold stocks for a short period of time, the tax structure is worse. The rates discussed here are for long-term capital gains.) What determines whether you pay 0, 15, or 23% on your capital gains? Your income level. The higher your income, the higher taxes you pay. This rate can be even more if you are a high income earner in a state like New York or California. In those states, you could easily be paying 30% or more of your capital gains to tax. So borrowing for income rather than selling shares makes more sense the richer you get.

As I write this text, our proud nation has fallen on desperate economic times, whether it feels that way on the street or not. Every single month our Federal Government spends much more than it takes in; the current fiscal situation is unsustainable due to ever growing mountains of national debt. Thus, we can reason that taxes are likely to go up sooner or later. People who pay 23% on capital gains income today could easily wind up paying 37% or more. Just to put that percentage in perspective, if you invest $100,000 and over time the value of your shares rises to $200,0000, then you will have to pay $37,000 in taxes when you sell.

Or you can just borrow against your shares and never sell them. In that case, you would pay 0% capital gains tax, because borrowed money is not considered income (since you will have to pay it back eventually).

This is not a solution for everyone. As the saying goes, it only works "when the stars align." There are two basic constellations that must be right. The macroeconomic situation of society must be right, and your personal situation must be right.

What Condition Your Condition Is In

The first element that must be right is the ratio of interest rates to the rates of return on your investments. In the 1980s, when interest rates were at 9 and 10%, and your stocks might return 8% or less, then this strategy would have made no sense. Today, qualified borrowers can get loans for 3% or less, and a conservative stock portfolio could return 7% or more. Under those circumstances, borrowing against stocks, rather than selling against stocks and triggering big taxes, starts to make sense.

This is especially true for dividend stocks. As we discussed earlier in the book, most people just earn 2 or 3% dividends on their stocks. By now, you should feel confident that you can earn 5 or 6% without breaking a sweat. If you borrow money at 3% interest against stocks paying a 6% dividend, the stocks pay the interest for you and the loan is basically free.

I say basically free because the money might still need to be repaid at some point. So this technique might not be right for everyone. It's only right for certain kinds of people in very specific circumstances.

The first circumstance might be if you are a traditional retiree advancing in age, or if you are generally in poor health. If, for whatever reason, you think you have less than ten years to live, you might be able to take the loan and never need to worry about paying it off while you're still above ground. If you are a high income person, that means you could be unlocking 37% more value to be used and enjoyed while you're still alive, because you can use more of your money without paying taxes on it. Upon your death, your estate will have to pay off the loan, but at that point you'll be beyond those kinds of earthly worries.

Another less grim scenario might be if you have many years left to live, but your income is lumpy. For example, I know several real estate brokers who happily live off borrowed money. They borrow against their assets to unlock tax free income, living off that money for months or even years. The whole time, they know they have large commissions coming to them, but they can't predict quite when. When the commissions do come in, the money is used to pay down the loan. If their operational bank account runs short, they then borrow against their assets to tide them over until their next big commission comes in. This approach allows them to be more patient in business, focusing on doing the right deals the right ways instead of worrying if they can pay their rent every month.

This approach can work for anyone who has an income that is large, but somewhat erratic or unpredictable. Some people receive unpredictable income from hedge funds, venture capital funds, or real estate projects. This lifestyle could even work for an actor or script writer who makes big, but irregular income from her creative work.

The other category of people where this might make sense are people with a borderline taxation status. Sometimes liquidation of securities can boost you into a higher tax bracket.

Let's say your regular income from your daily activities is $150,000. You have a paper profit of $250,000 in your stocks. Your daughter is getting married and you want to throw her a big party. But if you liquidate that large profit, you are going to trigger large taxes because the one-time, irregular profit will accidentally catapult you into a higher tax bracket. In these kinds of cases you might prefer to just borrow the money against your stock, and defer the big tax bill to another day.

Good Credit vrs Bad Credit

Credit and loans got a bad name in personal finance circles because most people have abused the privilege of credit and thus wound up with disastrous results. So-called "professionals" have also abused credit, for different reasons, and unleashed some infamously bad consequences. Credit is like fire; if you use it right, it will keep your shivering village warm throughout the cold night. If you use it wrong, you'll burn down the village. If your guts tell you that you could fall into the second group, then don't borrow anything at all. I built up my wealth for two decades before I began to explore this space.

The typical credit disaster involves credit cards. Credit cards are a terrible idea for two reasons. First, they charge absurd interest rates that actually would have been illegal throughout most of history. There is no such thing as a "good" loan at 19% interest. Second, they require regular payments that must be made on a dictated schedule. Any deviation from the dictated schedule triggers ruinous fees that bury consumers alive. All of these bad elements of credit cards stem from the fact that credit cards make unsecured loans. This means that huge corporations are making dubious loans to strangers with no assets to hold for collateral. Collateral is an asset that the lender holds as security to make sure they will be repaid. Would you make loans to a stranger with little legal recourse if they defaulted? Probably not, but if you did, you would demand outrageous interest rates and fees, because random lending is risky business.

What we were discussing above is secured lending, whereby you offer your stock as collateral. This dramatically changes the price of the loan and the terms of the loan. Currently I am able to borrow at less than 3% annual interest and I can pay back the loan whenever I feel like it. Compare that to 21% on your credit card with required payments every month. The cruel truth is: the richer you get, the easier it is to borrow money on great terms. If you get an asset based loan from your brokerage house, your interest rate will typically be determined by the size of your account. I know people with smaller brokerage accounts who are paying 5% for loans, and I know a few very rich people who have massive stock holdings who are paying as little as 1% to borrow money. When you have assets, you are the one with the advantage; don't be afraid to shop around and negotiate on price and terms.

That being said, there are still plenty of ways to set yourself up for disaster, even with asset based lending. That is typically where professional investors have gone terribly wrong in the past. They simply borrow too much. It's very possible to enjoy too much of a good thing. Remember the last time you had five glasses of champagne instead of just one or two? How did you feel the next morning?

Financial history is replete with cautionary tales of financial managers who borrowed too much, leaving their finances very fragile. You must remember that your relationship with your lender is very dependent on the condition of your collateral (in this case, your stock). Although we have already discussed many strategies to mitigate stock market risk, there will always be volatility, and even occasional stock market crashes. If you borrow $100,000 against $300,000 in collateral, and your portfolio crashes 30%, your collateral is still worth $210,000, which easily secures your $100,000 loan. However, if you borrow too much, say $250,000 against $300,000 in collateral, and your portfolio experiences the same stock market crash, suddenly the collateral will not secure the value of the loan anymore. Then your brokerage may automatically sell the underlying stock, paying off the loan and protecting themselves. Some version of this scenario is typically what causes financial empires to fall apart. The term is over leveraged. Basically, five glasses of champagne instead of just one. Don't borrow too much.

But how do you know what too much is? Everyone's situation is different and needs individual consideration. But a good general rule of thumb would be to follow the guidelines that closed-end fund managers must follow. Remember the Investment Company Act of 1940 that governs leverage and closed-end funds? That rule limits certain money managers to 33.3% leverage. In other words, if they have $3 in assets, $2 must be their own, and $1 can be borrowed. Remember, that is the maximum amount of leverage. Closed-end funds that use 33.3% are considered to be the most aggressive, most risky funds. Use that as your own personal benchmark. 33.3% is the maximum amount you could borrow against your stocks, but you should probably borrow less.

A Word About Margin

When discussing borrowing and stocks, terminology is important. What I have been discussing is asset based lending, i.e. using your stock as collateral so that you can take money out of your account, tax free, and spend a little.

The other kind of stock related borrowing is called margin. This is when you borrow money against your existing shares to buy more shares. This is a very common tactic in the high risk world of Wall Street, but I wouldn't recommend it for most regular retirees.

Why? Because margin investing can get complicated and risky fast. Most importantly, it doesn't necessarily help you build a stable, long term portfolio that yields passive income. Typically, people who buy stocks on margin are risk junkies who are trying to maximize short term price appreciation of their assets. It's a legitimate way to make money, with its own risks and rewards, but it's not necessarily going to help you create the steady passive income that a retiree should crave.

There is a reason why I put asset based lending at the end of this section of the book. It isn't for everyone. In fact, anyone considering this should consult with her own CPA or financial advisor about her own particular situation. However, if you think you'll live less than ten years, or you're a high income individual, or you are nervously waiting for that next commission check, it might make sense to borrow your income. Elon Musk famously lived off borrowed money for years because he didn't want to sell a single share of Tesla. While you may, or may not, achieve similarly electrifying results, ownership of assets is generally a good thing, and the techniques described above may help you unlock income without reducing ownership.

If you've made it this far in our book, you've now read 13 chapters, each one about a different way of generating growing passive income for yourself. You could think of this as 13 different pieces to a puzzle. We've taken each puzzle piece out of the box, looked it over carefully, and now we understand conceptually how the pieces might fit together.

But if you've ever worked with a puzzle before, you know that you don't really know anything until the hands-on fun begins. There is a big difference between studying the puzzle pieces and actually putting the thing together.

In the last part of this book, we will attempt to leave the theoretical and enter the practical. We will explore some real world case studies where you can meet people who are either building or reaping a retirement portfolio rich in passive income.

Who knows, maybe you will even recognize yourself! Whether you recognize yourself or merely recognize who you want to be, visualization is a powerful exercise.

As Walt Disney used to say, "If you can dream it, you can do it."

Part 3: The Real World

*All Characters represented in this section are fictional; for illustration purposes only.

Chapter 14: Sample Portfolio - The Kid

That perfect day in early June is still one of Meredith Johnson's favorite memories. She remembers the pins and needles she felt as she sat there in her black gown and scholar's cap. She held a little framed picture of her grandmother, which she intended to take on the stage with her when she accepted her diploma from her dean. Even though her grandma had recently passed away, just missing this great day in Meredith's life, she knew her grandma would be proud. After four years of hard work, her granddaughter would be graduating with a degree in computer science. It had amazed the matriarch that her grandbaby would have a college degree, and, of all things, was studying computers. Grandma had three children by age 22, and computers barely existed back then. Meredith's father operated a small plumbing business; after he and her mother divorced, her mother went to community college and got enough education to begin a career as an accounting assistant. Both her mother and father beamed up at her from the multitude of parents attending the graduation. Even though the two had barely spoken in a decade, on that day it almost felt like her family was back together again.

A number of prestigious corporations had come to campus to recruit promising graduates. Meredith had created her first resume with the guidance of the career office, and, despite trembling on the inside, had done well in her interviews. The result was an entry level job as an Information Technology Analyst at a well-known consulting firm. Although she had needed some loans to attend that four-year college, it seemed like all the hard work and risk was paying off. She and a college friend moved to Washington, D.C. together, sharing an apartment. The company that hired Meredith had an excellent training program, and she found that she was able to handle her new responsibilities without too much trouble. She even found a few colleagues at work that she could go to happy hour with. Everything was going to plan.

Well, almost everything, except for a nagging feeling. She tried pushing it down, but the feeling always came back. A stubborn voice in her head that whispered, "This isn't for you."

She liked computers. Her colleagues weren't too bad, and there were even a few that she liked. Her boss seemed reasonable, most of the time. But she just woke up every morning with that wind whistling through the back of her mind. The wind said, "What are you doing here?"

She tried to be a team player, and fit in, but she hated the endless conference calls and training sessions that seemed to just go in circles. She often had to work in teams, whether she actually needed the help or not. This was very annoying to her. While her boss never yelled at her outright, this boss was fond of spouting all kinds of sayings that made no sense, and it rankled Meredith to realize that her well being was so dependent on the whims of someone she really couldn't respect.

So, work was work. It wasn't the exciting world she had imagined on that perfect summer day when she walked across the stage to receive her diploma. But it wasn't terrible, either.

What was exciting was her dating life. When she first arrived in D.C., she went out with friends almost every weekend, and went to plenty of happy hours too. There were a few handsome guys in her life. Some she liked a lot more than others. But in the last year, she had been dating a guy she really liked, and things were getting serious. He was talking about them moving in together. But at 26, she wasn't a baby anymore, and she let him know that having a family was important to her. Even though the whole idea of moving in with him left her tingling with excitement, nothing was quite decided yet. Only time would tell.

For a Rainy Day

Meredith's mom and dad weren't financial geniuses, but they had done well enough after all. Dad still owned his plumbing business and Mom had worked her way up the accounting department and now reported to her company's VP of finance. Both of her parents had suffered through some rough financial years after the divorce. So, while they were kind of baffled by their daughter's new life as a young professional in the big city, they did both have the same piece of advice, "Honey, save some money now; it doesn't get any easier as you get older."

Meredith could see the wisdom of that advice. Afterall, she remembered going over to her newly divorced mother's house and finding an almost barren fridge. Also, there was that nagging feeling about her career. It really wasn't clear to her if she would move ahead in her company, or if she even wanted to move ahead in her company. Everything was going well enough, but it was hard for her to see herself attending Zoom meetings and corporate trainings for the rest of her life.

Additionally, she wasn't quite sure what would happen when she got married. Sometimes she needed to stay at the office until 7 or 8PM to get an important project done. Sometimes she needed to work most of Sunday to be ready for a meeting on Monday morning. How would she do that if she had two or three children? On one hand, she saw how her mother struggled for years after the divorce, so financial independence was important to her. But on the other hand, her older sister living in Northern

Virginia married a partner in a law firm, and was able to quit her job to raise her two children. Although Meredith's sister sometimes complained about lack of stimulation, it seemed like a pretty nice life to Meredith.

The bottom line was, she just wasn't sure exactly what her path would be. Was her current boyfriend "the one?" Would she work in Corporate America, or something more entrepreneurial? Or maybe her most important work would be raising a family? She felt torn and unsure about these questions. What was clear was what her dad told her, "More money saved means more options, honey."

So Meredith had resolved to build herself up financially and let the other questions work themselves out. That is why she split a two-bedroom apartment instead of renting her own apartment. Some people in D.C. had cars, but since she rarely left the city, it wasn't totally necessary. So she just took the Metro or Uber. She had seen friends spend thousands of dollars on clothes and handbags, but she mostly stayed away from that stuff. Otherwise she would have no income to save. Just living a modest existence in D.C. was expensive enough.

At age 26, Meredith made $70,000 before taxes. After taxes, health insurance and monthly contribution into her company's 401(k) program, she took home about $4,000 per month.

Of that $4,000 that she took home, $1,400 went to rent. Another $300 went to student loans. Roughly another $1,000 went to her food (Sunday brunch was a weekly social ritual with friends). Another $500 just disappeared somehow, going to expenses that just popped up. This left her with about $800 a month to invest (in addition to her 401(k) contribution).

What would be the smartest way for Meredith to invest if she wanted to maximize her financial security and flexibility in the decades to come?

Forging ahead with the 401(k)

Meredith had already taken the critical initial steps to establish a solid financial base for herself. She had limited her expenses, made progress towards paying off her educational debt, and not incurred any high interest rate credit card debt. During her first few years as a working adult, she saved up almost $20,000 in cash as an emergency fund. This way, if she got laid off for no fault of her own, she wouldn't have to go running back to her parents.

Even without fully understanding her future path, she was now in a position to begin building real wealth. If she ever wanted to quit her job and try something other than the corporate world, she would probably need several hundred thousand dollars in investments, if not even more. That may seem like a distant goal, but we'll soon see that some amount of financial independence would be achievable if Meredith invested wisely.

Let's start with her 401(k). This is a special investment account offered by her employer that offers some unique advantages. First, contributions to the 401(k) come directly from the top line of her paycheck; any amount that gets diverted from her paycheck does not get taxed. Furthermore, the money compounds inside of the account, tax free. Eventually, when Meredith withdraws the savings when she hits retirement age, the income will be taxed. But in the meantime, she could benefit from decades of powerful tax-free compounding. This means that the investments inside of the 401(k) could yield 2% dividends, or 12% dividends, but the income will just compound untaxed. For a dividend lover, this is a mouth-watering proposition.

Another huge benefit of the 401(k) account is that many employers match their employees contributions up to a certain limit. For example, some employers will pay $0.50 for every dollar you put in. Some match less, some match more. Really good employers will match your contribution $1 to $1 up to a certain limit.

Between the tax savings and the employer match, the 401(k) is a no brainer. However, there are three major pitfalls to avoid. First and foremost is fees.

In some circles, 401(k) plans have suffered from bad publicity, because sometimes employers don't do a good job of looking out for their workers. This has led to heart-breaking stories about unsophisticated employees being taken advantage of through high fees. While the match may come from your employer, the investments are often offered by a third party. The abuse happens when your employer neglects to negotiate a good deal regarding the management fees that the third party will charge. Good market rate fees should be 1% or less. However there are stories out there of unwitting employees paying fees of 2, 3 or even 4%, which would seriously harm their long-term returns. Since these embarrassing abuses have been revealed, many employers have gotten a lot tougher on negotiating fees for the third party investments that they offer. However, the person who will do the best job of looking out for you will always be you, so make sure to research the fees in your 401(k) before investing.

The second common pitfall can be over investment in company stock. The typical 401(k) will offer investment options such as the S&P 500 index, a growth index, or a bond index. It's also not uncommon for them to offer their own company stock, usually at preferential terms. This is often a popular option for 401(k) savers. They like the preferential terms on the stock purchase, and they feel comfortable buying company stock. They figure that, since they work at the company, they know a lot about the company and they believe in it's long-term prospects.

Sometimes this approach does work out great, but there are some tragic stories out there about workers who invested everything in their company stock, only to be totally wiped out decades after they ceased to work at the company. Remember Sears, RadioShack, and Kodak? They were all great companies that employees loved in the 80s and 90s. But if you had worked there from 1980 to 2000 and subsequently retired, you might well be living in poverty now. Additionally, some retirees have fallen victim to fraud; hundreds of thousands of Enron employees lost everything when it was revealed that the company was one of the largest frauds in American history.

It makes sense for you to want some ownership in the company you work in. It makes sense to believe in your company's mission. The problem is the lack of diversification. If you rely on your paycheck to support your family, and you also depend on that same company's stock to finance your old age, you just have a lot of exposure in one place. Consider a plan for financial diversification before you choose to put all of your 401(k) savings in your company's stock.

The last potential pitfall of a 401(k) is that it is really a traditional retirement vehicle. This means that once you put money in, it's hard to take money out until you hit age 59 ½. It's not impossible to take money out, but it's complicated and can trigger taxes and fees if done wrong. So, if you think you want to retire early, or you just want some funds that you can access easily, you might want to limit your 401(k) contribution to just the company match. For example, in many companies, your employer will match you $1 for $1 up to 3% of your salary. While you can still save tax free with additional amounts of your salary, your company won't match more than 3%. If you don't at least put in 3% of your salary, you are leaving your employer's free money on the table. But past that, how much more you put in depends on your goals.

Since the 401(k) would be the first investment that Meredith had ever made in her young life, she was a bit nervous. She converted this nervous energy into action, and she thoroughly researched her options. Since her future goals were somewhat unclear, she decided to put just 3% of her salary into her 401(k), so she could get her company's 100% match. This would mean that, before she earned $1 on her investments, she would be getting an automatic 100% return from her company.

But what investment to choose within the 401(k)? The plan didn't offer individual stocks; rather, most plan choices were different kinds of mutual funds. She could have chosen a fund that represented the S&P 500, the 500 largest stocks in the USA, she could have chosen a technology fund that specializes in high flying technology stocks, or she could have chosen an international fund, a fund that gains exposure to international stocks.

All three of the above would be fine choices, but she remembered that tax-free compounding. That means that every penny of dividend produced inside the fund just goes to buy more stock, growing the whole pie. Hard to get that kind of growth without special tax protection. So, she chose a dividend fund with less than a 1% fee. The fund yielded 4% and had delivered total returns of about 10% over decades.

Congratulations, Meredith! You just made your first simple step into the world of equity ownership. After she made her election, every biweekly paycheck saw a deduction of 3% of her gross pay. That 3% was matched by her employer. Remember, Meredith made $70,000 annually, pre-tax. So about $2,100 of this goes into the fund, and is promptly matched by another $2,100 from the company. With very little effort, Meredith was now saving $4,200 a year.

$4,200 a year in savings. Not bad at all for a young woman just starting out her life, but certainly a far cry from the quantities that she would eventually need to quit her job. With her future path uncertain, let's just see how these savings would add up over the next ten years.

We can use an investment calculator from www.smartasset.com. Other such calculators are easy to find on the internet, such as those offered by www.nerdwallet.com and even www.investor.gov.

If we assume that Meredith averages a 10% annual return on her 401(k) stock investment, and she keeps her contribution steady at $4,200 per year, then in ten years she will have amassed $77,831. Not bad at all, considering that she barely even notices the 3% taken out of her paycheck every two weeks. This projection also assumes that she will never get a raise, and never get promoted, which is unlikely for a bright young achiever like Meredith. If she gets promoted, and she makes more money, the 3% she puts in will automatically grow, and so will the match.

Meredith doesn't really love her job. But she does love her 401(k), and well she should. For as long as she chooses to stay on the corporate path, it's a great benefit.

To Roth, or Not to Roth? That Is The Question

That fact that she was doing nicely with her 401(k) did not deter Meredith from wanting to invest that extra $800 a month. In fact, once she jumped into the investment game with her 401(k), it only increased her confidence to take the next step.

The next question for her would be whether or not she should utilize a Roth IRA. A Roth IRA is a kind of retirement savings account that you can open up even if you already have a 401(k). You won't get all the same benefits as a 401(k), but the Roth still offers some neat tricks.

First off, the Roth IRA is an independent savings vehicle. You can put money in there, or not, but what you do is of your own initiative and your employer will probably not match that contribution.

You also won't get an immediate tax benefit. You may remember that the 401(k) contribution is made with *pre-tax* dollars. Unfortunately, that is not the case with the Roth IRA. Any funds that Meredith contributed to the Roth would have to come from the earnings she took home after her income taxes were paid.

But the Roth does offer one very special benefit. Whatever amount of money you amass over the years in your Roth will be *tax free* when you take it out in your old age. So, if you amass $100,000 in a Roth, and you take out $10,000 per year at age 60, that income will be untaxed. If you amass $1,000,000 in a Roth, and you take out $100,000 a year at age 60, then even that large amount will be untaxed. Not bad, not bad at all!

Additionally, the Roth provides the all-important tax-free compounding. Like the 401IK, any dividends you earn on money in the account just keep compounding. This makes the Roth a very friendly vehicle for dividend aficionados.

So then, obviously, Meredith should put all $800 per month into the Roth, right? Maybe. There are two caveats.

First, much like the 401(k), what goes in, can't come out. Well, it can come out, but not easily. If Meredith were dead set on a corporate career for the next forty years, with a standard retirement at age 67, then I would say that the Roth was a no brainer. But she doesn't have a crystal ball. What if she needed the money sooner?

Second, the Roth has some pretty low contribution limits. For 2021, the most you could legally put in there would be $6,000 per year. Since Meredith was projecting that she can put $800 per month into investments, even with her current modest financial situation she would max out quickly. If she got promoted over the years, she would quickly outgrow her Roth.

Her problem was her answer. Since she couldn't put the full $800 per month into the Roth anyhow, she might as well just put in half. So, each month, $400 went into the Roth IRA, and $400 went into a simple investment account that she opened on E-Trade.

This hybrid investment structure would also help diversify her investments somewhat. Since the regular account offered no tax protection, a young person such as herself could focus on pure growth. Remember, currently an investor pays no taxes on paper gains; she only pays on dividends or the sale of shares.

So, if Meredith developed a portfolio of high-flying tech stocks, she could double, triple, or quadruple her money without ever paying a dime of tax. She would only pay when she liquidates. She looked at a few different exchange traded funds that offered exposure to tech stocks, and ultimately she chose the QQQ. The QQQ is an exchange traded fund with a very low fee structure that offers exposure to the whole NASDAQ stock index. If you invested in the QQQ anytime over the last twenty years, it meant you rode the wave of unprecedented growth provided by companies such as Apple, Netflix, and Tesla. Nobody knows what the tech giants of tomorrow will be, but it's very likely that they will be listed on the NASDAQ. When Meredith chose the QQQ for her simple, taxable E-trade account, she chose maximum long-term growth prospects with minimum costs and taxes.

With her Roth account, she knew she had a better opportunity to leverage tax-free compounding of dividends. She hung out with some pretty motivated friends, many of whom have MBAs, and she asked around a bit. Some of her older friends pointed out to her that, since she was still somewhat young, she didn't need to find the stocks with the highest dividends. Instead, they thought that she needed to find the stocks with the highest *dividend growth.* Since she wasn't spending the dividends anytime soon (they were just going to pile up in her Roth), growth was the name of the game. (As we reviewed in Chapter 4).

Meredith explored her options. Remembering that she chose funds for her 401(k) and her regular account, she looked up some dividend growth funds. She found many offerings in this category, such as the iShares Core Dividend Growth (Ticker: DGRO) and the Vanguard Dividend Appreciation ETF (Ticker: VIG). These funds all have very low fees and offer broad exposure to a list of stocks that have grown dividends like clockwork for years, if not decades.

But now that she had success with her 401(k) and her E-Trade account, Meredith was feeling a little more gutsy. She was ready to pick a few individual stocks to buy and hold. Afterall, she was still young, so if she screwed up, she would have learned a lesson and would still have time to recover.

She took a few weeks and thought it over. What was a business that was always growing? She asked her dad. Now in his 50s, he said, "For some reason, my damn medicines always just cost more and more. They must be making money."

A light went on in Meredith's head. If pharma prices go up every year, they must make more and more money every year. After some research, she found that they do. Meredith came to realize that big pharmaceutical companies have been churning out ever higher dividends for decades. She bought shares in Pfizer (Ticker: PFE), Eli Lilly (Ticker: LLY) and Bristol Myers Squibb (Ticker: BMS).

After adding the Big Pharma stocks to her young portfolio, she waited a while before inspiration struck again. One day at happy hour with friends, she got into a conversation about what they missed from the suburbs. Most of her friends were crammed into apartments like her, and many didn't have cars, like her, and they only saw the suburbs when they went home to visit their parents.

One of her friends said, "I miss the $1.50 hotdog at Costco." Costco! It had been a while since she'd been to one of those, but then she remembered going with her mom in their SUV, and loading that thing to the brim with groceries, and not needing to go again for a month. Very different from how Meredith survived in D.C.

This recollection made Meredith curious, and she did some research. Turns out that Costco is well known for raising their dividend, and in fact, in recent years they'd raised their dividend by as much as 12% per year, essentially doubling their dividend every few years. So, Meredith added some Costco shares to her portfolio.

Lastly, her gut told her that she should buy some kind of "green" stock, something related to renewable energy. Her few friends who were interested in cars only wanted a Tesla or another electric car. At her job, she constantly received memos and newsletters celebrating the company's commitment to sustainable energy. Even her father, never the most progressive guy around, had mentioned that he was thinking about getting solar panels on the roof. She did some research and stumbled upon a company called Next Era Energy. This company owned a traditional utility business, and was also one of the biggest players in wind and solar energy nationwide. The name turned up on several internet lists she found of "fastest growing dividends." Soon, NextEra (Ticker: NEE) had a place in her portfolio as well.

So Meredith had begun her investing journey. Every month she put $400 in the QQQ exchange traded fund in the regular E-Trade Account. Every month she put $400 in the Roth IRA, dividing the $400 amongst the five stocks named above. When cash dividends entered her Roth account, which happened every three months, she simply reinvested those dividends in more shares. Sometimes the share values went up; sometimes the share values went down. She barely noticed. She didn't know where the future would take her, but she was committed to investing for the long haul.

What would Meredith's picture look like if we took the same view that we took of her 401(k)? Let's say she achieved a 10% annual return on both her E-Trade account and her Roth account. Remember, this could mean that one account only hit 8%, while the other hit 12%. It could also mean that some years were way down, while other years were way up. But, after 10 years, let's say she achieved an annualized return of 10%. That would be fairly in line with what the stock market has produced over long periods of time.

If Meredith put in $800 a month, after just ten years, she would have $177,899!

For a young woman under forty, who had started with almost nothing, Meredith would have a net worth approaching $250,000 by age 36.

For someone who isn't quite sure what the future holds, $250,000 means a lot of options. If she decides to take some time off from work to raise a family, she can do so without being penniless and helpless. If she wants to take a shot at something entrepreneurial, she can try that without risking total financial disaster.

For a 26-year-old woman with an active love life and a promising career, the sky's the limit. A successful marriage may reinforce her growing wealth, or she may be unlucky in love, and take the financial stress that comes with that setback. She may start a small business that becomes a large business, or she may fail again and again at entrepreneurship. Anything could happen. But at age 26, she certainly has set herself up to take control of her own future.

Let's just explore one possibility for fun. Let's say that Meredith marries, has children, and maintains her employment exactly as it is today. She never really moves up the corporate ladder, but she doesn't get pushed off, either. She gets only marginal raises to keep up with inflation. Her husband contributes financially, but only modestly so. She remains frugal, so she keeps up the very same investment regime described in this chapter. Except, in this theoretical word, she keeps it up for 30 years, from age 26 to age 56.

In that case, her 401(k) would be worth $764,162. Her Roth and regular E-Trade account would be worth $1,746,657. At age 56, Meredith would be looking at a robust and early retirement, even if her husband contributed little and she never made any progress in Corporate America. That's the astounding power of dividends and compounding. The secret is not being a great stock picker, or the smartest girl on the block. The secret is simple consistency and time.

If you, or someone you love, has an opportunity to start investing early, please encourage that possibility. It made all the difference in the world for our fictional Meredith; it can make a very real difference for you as well.

TABLE 1: MEREDITH JOHNSON'S FINANCES (ANNUAL)

Pre-Tax Income	$70,000
Take Home Pay	$48,000
Rent	-$16,800
Student Loan	-$3,600
Food/Entertainment	-$12,000
Miscellaneous	-$6,000
Remainder to Save	$9,600
Total Savings Including 401(k)	$13,800

Growth of Meredith Johnson's Savings

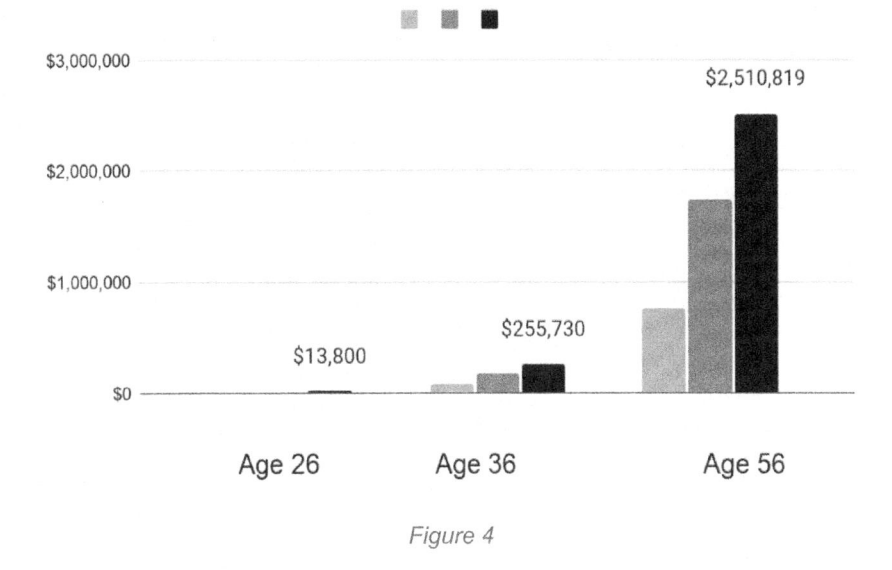

$3,000,000

$2,510,819

$2,000,000

$1,000,000

$255,730

$13,800

$0

Age 26   Age 36   Age 56

Figure 4

    The chart above shows the growth in Meredith's savings, assuming she contributes at a steady rate, earns a 10% compounded total return, and never saves any more than what she started saving at age 26. The three bars represent her 401(k), her Roth and regular E-Trade account, and her total savings. (Total savings are the black bar; light grey is the 401K and dark grey is the Roth IRA+regular savings).

Suggested Investments for Meredith Johnson

Roth IRA, Individual Dividend Stocks
30.0%

401K, Dividend Growth Fund
40.0%

Regular E-Trade, QQQ (Nasdaq Fund)
30.0%

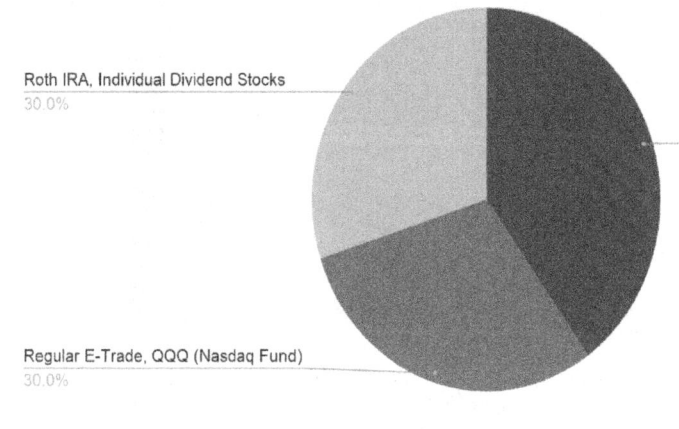

Figure 5

Chapter 15: Model Portfolio - The Professional

If you asked Marcus Jackson to describe his family in just one word, he would say "hardworking." For as long as he could remember, everyone in his family had at least two jobs. His dad worked construction during the week, which was good, steady work as the Atlanta metro area just kept growing, and then worked as a handyman on nights and weekends. His mom worked as an aide at a nursing home during the week, and then on weekends would work as a private helper for rich older folks. His grandma lived in his house growing up and kept an eye on the kids while Mom and Dad were working. He could just barely remember his grandfather; he died young from a heart attack, and Marcus's mother always used to say that working too much killed him.

No matter how hard everyone was working, the family always made time to go to church. That was Grandma's favorite day. Marcus can still remember her carefully pressing and ironing her Sunday best. In some ways, church was awfully boring for a little kid, but Marcus remembers loving those times because it was one of the few times when the whole family was together. He also remembers the feeling of dread on Sunday night; he knew that soon his mom and dad would go back to work and he wouldn't see them much during the week.

His absolute favorite time as a kid was Sunday afternoon, after church. The family would sit around the supper table with hot steaming food piled high. This was Marcus's time to shine. His parents wanted to know everything about school. Which teachers did he like? Did he learn anything interesting this week? How did the other kids treat him? School was alright, but mostly Marcus loved all the attention. After discussing his latest report card, his mother would take him in her arms, and rock him just like she had when he was a baby; she talked about a place called "college." She said it would all be worth it when her baby grew up and went to college. Young Marcus didn't quite understand what that place was, but if it made Mom happy, then he was going.

Marcus did go to college. He was the first person in his family to attend college and graduate with a degree. Due to his parents' many years of hard labor, the family was able to pool their resources to make just enough for Marcus to graduate with no loans. He had been a top student in his high school, which also helped him score some partial scholarships.

His mom cried at graduation and she said that she knew her father, who had worked himself to death as a janitor, was smiling down from heaven.

Marcus got a degree in accounting and began his career as a junior accountant at one of the big firms downtown. Although he had just barely made it out of college with no debt, he didn't have much other than a used suit he bought at Goodwill and a beat up old Honda that his uncle had given him. So, Marcus decided to get ahead the only way he knew how: hard work.

That first decade in Atlanta, Marcus took any assignment he could get his hands on. Did a vice president need someone to prepare a report on a Sunday? Call Marcus. Did some urgent firm business come up on Christmas Eve? Call Marcus. Did something critical come up during Marcus's scheduled vacation? That's fine, Marcus would just cut the vacation short and get back to work.

His hard work and dedication started to pay off as he slowly but surely got promotions at the accounting firm. But

Marcus had bigger ambitions. Somehow, some way, he just knew he wanted to work for himself. Sometime around his 35th birthday, he had finally amassed the capital and the guts to make the big leap. With just a couple of his own clients lined up, Marcus resigned from the big firm downtown and put up his own shingle: "Marcus Jackson, CPA."

Around the same time, something else very special happened. He met Monique. After some old college friends twisted his arm, he took some rare time off of work to attend a concert with a group. And Monique was there, looking fine. His heart skipped a beat.

Not only was Monique beautiful, but she was also a hard worker. Just like Marcus. She was also the first college graduate in her family, and she worked as a nurse in a well known local hospital. In fact, Monique had started out as a nursing assistant, and eventually put herself through college at night while working full time. Monique attracted Marcus like a magnet; not only was she beautiful, but she was a hustler!

Soon, they were married, and Marcus not only had a new firm of his own, but soon two babies of his own as well.

Those first few years were some of the toughest of his life. Not only was he in charge of business development and marketing, but now he was also his own chief financial officer and secretary. Oh, yeah, at some point someone had to do the actual accounting work as well. Monique's income and benefits as a nurse were critical for his family's survival those first few years. Even though their families helped out with child care, between babies crying all night and adult clients crying like babies, from age 35 to 40, Marcus only slept five hours a night.

Once again, hard work and courage started to pay off for Marcus. By his early 40s, his life started to stabilize. His fledgling firm started to attract richer clients. Richer clients meant more complex accounting needs, with more in depth consulting needs. Now Marcus wasn't just some guy who prepared taxes once a year. Marcus was starting to work himself into a position where wealthy people in the Atlanta area looked at him as a trusted counselor and advisor on accounting and taxation matters.

It was around this time, in his early 40s, that a revelation came to Marcus that rocked his world. He noticed it with his first few wealthy clients, but the pattern became more and more pronounced. Eventually, the pattern became so obvious that the realization was undeniable.

His clients did not work hard. In fact, many barely did anything at all. One client had to take a year off from work altogether for cancer treatment, and during that year of not working, his income was the largest it had ever been due to stock and real estate investments. Many of his clients were widows or ex-wives who had lived off investments for decades without ever doing anything more than volunteer work.

At first, he paid no mind; he just did the taxes, and collected the fees. But as he grew closer and closer with some big clients, the realization was inescapable. His richest clients did very little work, because they had *everyone else working for them.*

It was a bitter pill to swallow at first. He thought of his grandfather, falling over dead one day while mopping a floor. He thought of the tears in his mother's eyes when she explained why she had to miss an event at Marcus's school. Marcus was good at math; he knew darn well that a lot of these rich folk made more in a month doing nothing than his mom had made in a year working her fingers to the bone.

But his second epiphany was even more important than the first. It took some soul searching and some consideration, but once the idea crept into his brain, there was no going back. If his rich clients could set themselves up for a life of leisure, so could he. They possessed no magic abilities that set them apart from Marcus. They had just been born into different circumstances, or had made a few very good moves in business. A few had just gotten lucky.

But Marcus was smart. Marcus had been born into modest circumstances, but positioned himself with a clear view into how the other half lived. And he could be just as lucky as the next guy if he made his own luck.

What Marcus and Monique needed was a plan. A plan by which they could start working less and making more. A plan by which they could sleep more than five hours a night. A plan by which they could take control of their own lives without falling over dead from a heart attack in a conference room somewhere.

Marcus and Monique started talking, and started planning. Soon, they decided to make some big changes.

A Plan is Born

When Marcus and Monique started to plot out their future in earnest, Marcus was 42 and Monique was 36. They had two children, ages 5 and 3. The couple had both been pretty good savers before they met each other and after, so they had around $200,000 in 401(k) accounts. As we have discussed previously, both Marcus and Monique had taken advantage of generous corporate matching contributions when they could. They also had about $75,000 in home equity, and a few thousand dollars saved for the children's future college education. Marcus was proud of his family's savings. Not bad at all for a guy who had nothing but lint in his pockets at age 22!

As happy as he was with his progress, he knew he still had a long way to go if he wanted his investments to pay him a monthly passive income that could replace his working income. Part of the challenge was simply that, between his growing accounting practice and Monique's income from nursing, his family had a pretty good income. High current income meant he would need a lot of assets to replace that income.

Marcus was making roughly $160,000 from his accounting business. If Monique worked full time at the local hospital, she could make $65,000 plus healthcare benefits for the whole family. This would give his family a pre-tax income of $225,000. After taxes, the family took home roughly $180,000.

The couple spent roughly $4,500 per month on housing. That was mortgage, taxes, and insurance. If you factored in maintenance as well, that was at least another $500 per month. With both he and Monique working full time, nobody had time to fix things around the house, or to mow the lawn. They just hired people to do those jobs.

The second biggest family expense was day care. That cost about $1200 a month for the two kids. Even though Marcus and Monique had a loving family that could help out with the kids one or two days a week, Marcus didn't expect his mother to raise his kids the way his grandmother had raised him. His mom had diabetes, arthritis, and high blood pressure; she barely scraped by every month with a part-time job and her social security check. Marcus wouldn't feel comfortable with the family's elder generation caring for his kids full time.

The third biggest expense was the two family cars. Safety was important to Marcus, and no one really knew how to fix a car, so he didn't want anyone driving used up old beaters (he had enough stories about his uncle's old Honda to entertain friends for hours). But they didn't need luxury either. So, Marcus drove a new Toyota while Monique drove the family minivan. Monthly cost? About $1200 including insurance and gas.

This meant that his family had about $7400 per month in "hard" expenses. These were expenses that were pretty much fixed and were predictable every month. Or about $88,800 per year against their post tax income of $180,000.

Food costs about $1,000 a month. Another $1,000 went towards entertainment, vacation, or whatever. So the family spent about $112,000 a year of the $180,000 that came in post-tax. As long as everyone kept working hard, they were in a good financial position.

But the work came with a price. One weekend, after working all day from Monday to Saturday, he was awakened at 6AM on Sunday by his kids toddling into his room and jumping on his bed with cries of "Daddy, aren't you awake?" Of course this was irritating given that Sunday was, theoretically, his one day to sleep in. But mostly, he was just baffled. Weren't these two just babies in their cribs? Now they were walking and talking and getting into trouble just like little people. What happened? Where did the time go? Marcus had been working six days a week as long as he could remember. Why was he spending six days a week taking care of someone else's family?

After talking it through, and working out the numbers together, the couple decided on the following. Starting immediately, Monique would cut back her hours and work part time. She would work just enough so that she could still get those valuable healthcare benefits from her job. But she would keep working; in case she got bored, or if the family wound up with unexpected financial problems, she could always go back full time. Marcus would continue working as much as needed to build up his firm, but the family would make a commitment to cultivate passive income through rigorous saving and investing. Marcus figured that, if he did things right, the passive income would supplement his family's active income, and he could cut back to working just four days a week by age 50. This way, he would never have to explain to his kids why he was missing their baseball games.

An Active Plan for Passive Income

When Monique slashed her hours at the hospital, the following changes occurred in the family's finances. The total post tax income was reduced from $180,000 to $160,000, but the daycare expense was also cut in half to $7,200. So now the family spent around $105,000 a year against income of $160,000 of take home pay.

This left a meaty $55,000 a year to invest. Since Marcus wanted to enjoy the passive income from these investments sooner rather than later, the money went into regular, taxable accounts. They calculated that they could leave the $200,000 in their 401(k)s untouched and it would eventually grow into a substantial retirement fund all on its own. The funds they were aiming to build up now were to help pay for a "semi-retirement."

Where to invest? How to invest? The money in the 401(k) had just gone into a S&P 500 index fund; it was the most simple answer. But now the couple specifically needed income. Even though Marcus had already spent two decades moving numbers around for those rich clients, he was still a bit intimidated at first. Although he considered himself an expert on other people's finances, he had never really thought so much about his own.

One clear pattern that had emerged from his exposure to the affluent set was that many had done very well with real estate. Some owned apartment buildings, others had owned shopping centers. More often than not, they did quite well over time. However, as a consultant and counselor, he also knew more than a few clients who had gotten sucked into hairy situations related to maintenance and management of their properties. The whole concept of the couple's new plan was to work *less,* not more. So, direct ownership of real estate was out.

This led Marcus to investigate REITs (which we covered in Chapter 8). The more he read, and the more he broke down the accounting statements of these publicly traded companies, the more he felt he could get a lot of the same benefits of direct ownership, without the hassles. So, he and Monique agreed to put 30% of their annual investment money into REITs. In this allotment, they chose the Vanguard Real Estate ETF (Ticker: VNQ) and a few individual REITs based on their particular interests. Monique had spent many years working in hospitals, so they felt comfortable investing in a REIT that owns hospitals, Medical Properties Trust (Ticker: MPW). Marcus had known many clients who got rich renting simple, affordable apartments, so they bought AIMCO (Ticker: AIV) and AvalonBay Communities (Ticker: AVB). As an accountant, Marcus was also very attuned to the need for storage of records, both paper and digital. So he chose Iron Mountain, a company that specializes in document storage and digitization, (Ticker: IRM).

Using information that was readily available on his E-Trade account, Marcus could calculate that this part of his portfolio would yield an average of around 5% annually. But while he was doing his research, there were other REITs that stood out because they paid more, *much* more. In fact, it seemed like they paid too much. If most REITs paid 4 or 5%, how could these other REITs be paying 10%?

This discrepancy awakened the beancounter in him, and he decided to comb through a few of the companies' annual reports. This is when he discovered that the higher paying REITs were actually a different kind of REIT. They were mortgage REITs. (We explored mortgage REITS in chapter 9). They paid a higher income because they were a different kind of business. Although both businesses were classified as REITs, it was apples to oranges, really.

He talked it over with Monique, and no matter how he made the argument, it just smelled wrong to her. They paid too much. It must be too risky. After a few heated conversations, the couple settled on the following compromise. They would put 10% of their monthly investment money in mortgage REITs, and then only the largest, most established company. If it went OK, then they would try more over time. The next day, Marcus went onto his E-Trade account and bought shares in Annaly Capital Management (Ticker: NLY), the largest mortgage REIT. This investment was yielding around 9%.

As a nurse, Monique felt comfortable with the idea of investing in pharmaceutical stocks. That whole world was foreign to Marcus, so he completely let her control this portion of their investments. He let her do the research, and then she told him which companies she preferred. It was honestly a relief to hand some of the hard work off to someone else on his "team." On Monique's recommendation, they bought shares in Pfizer (Ticker: PFE), Abbvie (Ticker, ABBV), Novo Nordisk (Ticker: NVO) and Johnson&Johnson (Ticker: JNJ). Although some of these companies paid lower dividends than the REITs, Marcus could see that they had a stellar track record of growing their dividends. In fact, they had often doubled the dividend every ten years or so. This would mean that, if his family came to rely on the dividend income, he could also count on a pay "raise" every year. Not a bad deal; he certainly couldn't say the same for his own business. The Big Pharma component would be 30% of their monthly investments.

70% of their monthly investments were now allotted. When he thought of the very richest clients who had walked into his accounting firm, Marcus thought of borrowed money. Not the bad kind. Not the kind to buy bigger houses and fancier cars. Rather, the kind to buy more apartment buildings or double the size of a small business. He recalled a feeling of amazement when looking over the books and records of these particular clients. They made a lot of money, fast, by using other people's money.

However, he had been doing it long enough that he had also seen a few high rollers crap out in the leverage game. He saw a few real estate developers lose everything after years of work. It was tempting to go for it anyway, but Monique reminded him that the point of the whole portfolio was to *reduce* stress, not ramp it up.

There had to be a middle way, a way of taking advantage of the astounding power of leverage while still sleeping at night. That was when Marcus discovered closed-end funds.

He read about the concept in Kipplinger's Magazine, a finance publication that he had subscribed to years ago. (We learned about closed end funds in Chapter 12). For the longest time, he got weekly newsletters from them in his email, which he never made the time to read. When he forced himself to start reading, amazing things started to happen. One of those amazing things was his realization that closed end funds fit the description of what he was looking for.

He wound up starting out with a shotgun approach. He bought a few different closed-end funds, each one with a different specialty. He figured that this bought him some protection in diversification, and it also allowed him to maximize his learning. He bought a fund that specialized in infrastructure, the Cohen & Steers Infrastructure Fund (Ticker: UTF). He bought another fund that specialized in high yielding international dividend stocks, the Aberdeen Global Dynamic Dividend Fund (Ticker: AGD). He even bought a fund that specialized in bonds (The Double Line Income Solutions Fund, Ticker: DSL). He figured this was one area where he could benefit from professional management, since he knew little about fixed income. All and all, he calculated that this part of his portfolio should throw off a monthly income of around 8% of the initial purchase price.

Sowing and Harvesting

Within a year of beginning their plan, the Jackson family had a diversified portfolio of high yielding stocks. The average yearly yield was about 6%. So, on that first $55,000 invested, they earned about $3,300 of passive income. It wasn't much, but Marcus's heart raced the first few months when dividends appeared in his brokerage account, as if by magic. After all those years of busting his rear for every penny, here was money that just fell from the sky. Astounding.

Marcus and Monique went into their plan understanding that anything could happen. At age 42, Marcus had taken enough hard knocks in life to know that no one has a crystal ball. But his mathematical nature just couldn't resist making some calculations on what his life *could* look like on his 50th birthday.

His assumption would be that all dividends would be reinvested until his 50th birthday. If the dividends had been in a tax-sheltered retirement account, he might have used a compounding rate of 10%. But that would have meant that he could not access the funds until age 59 ½. So, he planned to "Render Unto Caesar," which would reduce his effective compounding rate to 8%. Even at that rate, if he continued to salt away $55,000 a year between age 42 and age 50, he would have amassed $686,000.

At age 50, that $686,000 could provide $41,160 if he continued to receive a 6% yield. Remember, based on the costs that Marcus analyzed earlier, that passive income could easily cover the cost of his family's cars and their annual vacation.

It's possible that, after eight years of experience, Marcus and Monique would feel comfortable investing in more high yielding securities, like mortgage REITs or more aggressive closed-end funds. So, perhaps they could receive income of 8% on their $686,000 instead of 6%. At that rate, their investments would throw off $54,880 of pure passive income. In that scenario, Monique could quit her nursing career altogether if she wanted, or Marcus could simply stop taking phone calls on Saturday.

If the Jacksons start to enjoy that passive income at age 50, does that mean that they are sacrificing tomorrow in order to work less today? Not necessarily.

Remember, the Jacksons already had $200,000 in 401(k)s plus home equity. The whole time, that money is growing untouched. What financial position would the couple be in at age 67?

If they had $200,000 in their 401(k) at age 42, and it achieved a 10% compounded return (tax-sheltered) in the 401(k), then they would have $2,166,000 in the accounts when Marcus hits traditional retirement age. At the same time, they would have their additional $686,000 portfolio that they began tapping at age 50. Except, in this case, the dividend income has grown at an annual rate of 6%, meaning that the cash flow has *tripled* between Marcus's 50th birthday and his 67th birthday. The portfolio that paid $41,160 in passive income on Marcus's 50th birthday would pay roughly $123,000 on his 67th birthday.

Even as companies have been raising the dividends, the share prices have slowly been increasing as well. If we assume that the share prices grow at just 3% per year, the securities themselves would be worth roughly $1,133,000 on his 67th birthday, *even though Marcus has been spending the dividends for years.*

Even if the Jacksons begin to tap their passive dividend income when Marcus turns 50, it's quite possible that they will be looking at a retirement income in excess of $200,000 in their old age.

The Jackson family has traveled a long, long way from the days when Marcus's grandfather worked two jobs until his heart stopped beating. They've gone from working for income to having others work to provide income for them. They may not have direct contact with their employees, but each stock they own represents a dedicated management team and thousands of employees working to make the Jackson family rich every day. If you hold corporate shares, then these same managers and employees can work to make your family rich, too.

TABLE 2: Jackson Family Finances (In Annual Numbers)

Old Plan	New Plan
Total Family Income: $225,000	$205,000
Post Tax: $180,000	$160,000
Housing costs -60,000	Housing costs -$60,000
Daycare -$14,400	Daycare -$7,200
2 Cars -$14,400	2 Cars -$14,400
Food -$12,000	Food -$12,000
Entertainment -$12,000	Entertainment $-12,000
Total spent: $112,800	Total spent: 105,600
Total left to invest: 67,200	Total left to invest: $54,000

Jackson Family Passive Income Growth

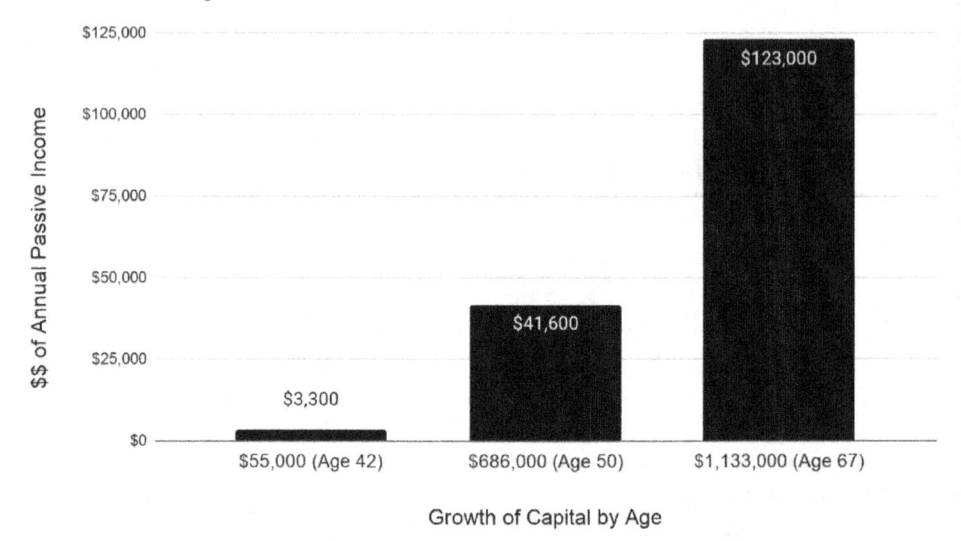

	$55,000 (Age 42)	$686,000 (Age 50)	$1,133,000 (Age 67)
Annual Passive Income	$3,300	$41,600	$123,000

Growth of Capital by Age

Figure 6

This chart assumes that the Jackson family invests $55,000 per year starting at age 42 with a compounded annual rate of return of 8%. At age 50, Marcus starts to withdraw and spend the dividends and contributes no more money. Between age 50 and age 67, the portfolio produces a 6% dividend, which Marcus spends. By age 67, with no further contributions, the portfolio has grown to $1,133,000 and throws off about $123,000 in annual income.

Suggested Investments for the Jackson Family

Diversified Closed End Funds
30.0%

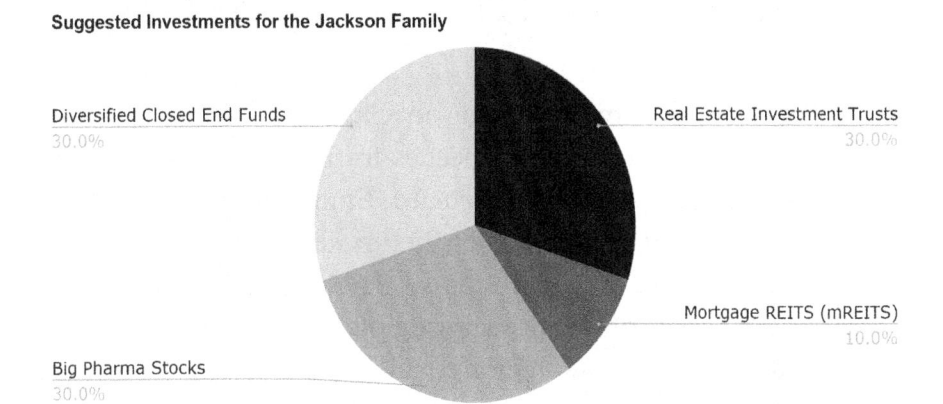

Real Estate Investment Trusts
30.0%

Mortgage REITS (mREITS)
10.0%

Big Pharma Stocks
30.0%

Figure 7

Chapter 16: Model Portfolio - The Pre-Retiree

Early April meant spring in Charlotte, North Carolina, and spring meant barbecues for the Smith family. And why not? Afterall, Mitchell J. Smith and his wife Gracie had worked hard to afford their luxurious, six bedroom, 5,500 square foot home on a golf course. He had put in thirty years working for some of the more prestigious companies in America, eventually becoming a regional sales manager for a medical device company. Gracie had tackled the tough task of raising two beautiful daughters while also working as a pharmaceutical representative. She had never moved up, but she had always been happy and well paid as an individual sales contributor for her employer.

Because they had spent so long in the medical sales world, a lot of their social acquaintances were also from that world. In fact, Mitchell and Gracie's best friends, the Smeads, were also long term medical sales pros. Barney Smead was a sales manager just like Mitchell, and Raquel was an accomplished pharma rep just like Gracie. The two couples had a lot of fun over the years comparing "war stories" from their days in the corporate trenches.

But today was all about fun. After being bundled away all winter, the industrial size, stainless steel grill was fired up with some prime meats from the local boutique butcher. The aroma of sizzling beef tickled Mitchell's nose as he poured his first drink of the day for himself and Barney.

A few families stood around and chattered blithely as they enjoyed the direct view from the home's teak wood deck onto the golf course. Nothing today but blue skies and balmy breezes; it felt like winter had ended a million years ago.

But somehow, Barney just wasn't himself. One reason why Barney had done so well as a sales manager was his gift of gab. Normally, Barney would be the life of the party, always getting the conversation going with some kind of jovial story. But today he wandered around the deck silent and ashen, just barely following whatever conversations were percolating.

Mitchell put his arm around Barney and walked him to the edge of the deck, away from the others. "How ya feelin' today, Barn?" Mitchell inquired.

"Not great. Not great at all, to tell you the truth. They shitcanned me, Mitch. Twenty five years and they shitcanned me like some punk."

Mitchell recoiled as if he had seen a snake hissing in the bushes.

"Seriously? Didn't you just win manager of the year last year?" Mitchell asked.

"Yup, manager of the year, 2019. You know how many of those awards I won over the years? And now, three months severance and 'good luck'. Shit, my kids aren't even done with college yet. And all they tell me is 'good luck.'"

The shocking news reverberated around Mitchell's head like an errant bullet, damaging every point that it hit. It really wasn't surprising news. He had seen dozens of good reps and managers laid off over the years, seemingly at random. But it had never hit this close to home. Shit, Barney lived in a house just like his right in the next development down the road.

"Awww. Screw 'em, Barn. You've got a string of awards a mile long, I'm sure you'll find something new in no time. Maybe even something better," Mitch threw his arm around Barney's shoulders as the pair gazed out onto the endless manicured green of the golf course. "This will just mean the beginning of something new for you, Barn."

The words tasted like acid before they even came out of Mitchell's mouth. The beginning of something new, for sure. But of what? Barney had some big bills to pay. Between his $2,000,000 mortgage, his two kids in private college, and the fact that he supported his elderly in-laws, Barney had confessed to him in the past that he and Raquel didn't have much in the bank. It was true that Barney had a long track record of success as a sales manager, but at age 56, Mitchell wasn't really sure if that would work for Barney or against him. At age 58, Mitchell was usually the oldest sales manager in the room when he attended corporate meetings. Even he would admit, strictly in confidence, that he typically did not like to hire or manage reps who were older than 40-something. They just didn't seem to have the drive of the younger reps.

And of course, in the deep dark recesses of Mitchell's mind, well out of sight of his everyday thoughts, a nasty little voice scoffed, "If Barney is screwed at age 56, then what about you at age 58?" He tried to banish the voice before his appetite was ruined by a wave of nausea. Well, maybe Barney hadn't done a good job of saving, but the Smith family would be A-OK. Mitch and Gracie had about $500,000 in 401(k) plans, and about another $500,000 in this $2,000,000 home. They would probably be just fine whenever their careers ended.

Still, Mitchell had to admit that things were changing around him. The youngest of his two daughters was finally graduating from college; that would free up a substantial chunk of change. The culture of the medical sales business was rapidly changing; going way downhill in Mitchell's opinion. In the old days, it was all about building relationships with doctors and administrators. Luxurious golf rounds, fishing trips, and concerts with clients were the norm. Now, if you gave the wrong person a free pen, HR would be up your ass. Mitchell was getting pretty darn tired of the whole thing.

His daughter was finishing college, and with this thunderbolt from Barney, maybe it was time to meet with a financial advisor. He felt sure that half a million in 401(k)s meant his family was on track, but you never could be too sure. As he patted a palid Barney on the back, he resolved to make an appointment with that advisor who had been recommended to him.

In the meantime, it was time for that next scotch. Better make it a double.

An Inconvenient Truth

A month later, the Smiths sat down with Bill Anderson, a financial advisor that had been recommended by Mitchell's cousin. They hadn't had a meeting like this in a long time.

Bill proposed the following method. First, to discuss just the raw numbers behind their financial life, and then to discuss the "why?" behind some of their investment concepts and spending. That seemed logical to Mitch; he ran annual reviews with his sales employees in a similar manner.

For starters, Mitchell earned about $230,000 annually in his job as a regional sales manager. As about 30% of his pay was variable incentive that depended on his team's performance, that number could fluctuate up or down. But the average was around $230,000. He had earned that average, adjusted for inflation, for many years.

Gracie earned roughly $110,000 as a pharmaceutical representative. She also could see some variation, but $110,000 was typically her target number.

Together, the couple earned $340,000 pre-tax. They also got two brand new, if utilitarian, company vehicles to drive. Additionally, both got great health insurance as part of their jobs. Although there was a monthly cost deducted from Mitch's paycheck, that cost was much lower than if he were self-employed, and his deductibles and copays were reasonable during the rare occasions when he needed medical attention.

Boy, that seemed like a lot of money. Mitchell's own father had been a school teacher. If he were still alive today, he would have considered Mitchell to be rich.

But then taxes happened. Between federal, state, and social security taxes, the Smith's actually took home much less than they earned on the top line of their paychecks. Additionally, Mitch's two daughters, age 21 and 26, were also on his corporate insurance. While Mitch was grateful for this benefit, it still meant a chunk of money came out of his check every month. All and all, the Smith family only took home around $220,000 of the $340,000 that they earned every year.

Next Bill and the Smiths went over expenses. Mitch's home was his castle, and castles don't come cheap. His monthly mortgage payments, plus taxes and insurance, could add up to $90,000 a year. After Bill gently twisted his arm, Mitch had to admit that maintenance cost at least another $10,000 a year.

This winter, and most winters, the Smith's spent time in their ski cabin in the mountains. That cost about $30,000 a year after mortgage payments and everything else were factored in.

The couple had driven to the appointment in a convertible Porsche. Even though the company provided two new vehicles for the couple to drive, no one was going to get a thrill out of a Buick SUV with a basic trim package. The truth was, most corporate fleet cars were makes or models that the manufacturers had tried and failed to sell to the general public. Not very fun to drive. So Mitch and Gracie had decided to live a little and leased the Porche for $1,000 a month.

Next were their daughters. Even though the two hadn't lived in the 5,500 square foot Smith home for quite a while, they still got plenty of support. Jennifer, the youngest daughter, went to a private college that cost around $40,000 a year. The elder daughter, Samantha, had graduated from a similar private college.

The Smiths were very loving, giving parents. Some of Mitchell's very favorite memories were his little daughters running around the big house. He would shake his head in amazement, "where did all the time go?" He knew he wanted the best for his daughters. And that meant the best education. Mitchell himself had barely gotten into any college at all, and that was mostly just because he had been a football player. If his daughters did well enough in school to go to a private college, then it was Mitch's responsibility to pay for it.

He was very proud to have been able to put his daughters through good schools without them taking on a penny of debt. His own situation was different. He went through a rough patch about midway through Samantha's schooling, and the commissions just didn't come in the way they were supposed to. What was he going to do, suddenly ask his 20-year-old daughter to drop out of school, leaving behind the only world she had ever known? Ask her to take on loans before she was even old enough to buy a beer? No, instead Mitch and Gracie had taken out a modest educational loan, to be paid back over ten years. They had never even told Samantha. Now that loan payment was about $7,000 a year.

Mitch would never regret paying for his daughters' education. But that didn't mean he was happy with Samantha. After majoring in anthropology, she had never really been able to secure a good job after graduation. She had worked at an independent book store, worked as a docent in a museum, and now she was a barista at an independent, organic, fair trade coffee shop. It seemed like every time she came by the house to ask for more money, she had more and more tattoos. The last time she had stopped by she introduced someone named "Yor" as her partner. Mitch and Gracie struggled to figure out if Yor was a man, a woman, or something else. They were afraid to ask. Apparently there were more than two options on that front, these days.

At any rate, no one wanted to talk about it, but in the comforting space of Bill Anderson's office, Gracie admitted that she gave around $1,000 a month to Samantha, her 26-year-old daughter.

After that, their family spent about $10,000 per year on food, and $10,000 on entertainment and miscellaneous expenses.

The numbers were pretty plain as Bill wrote them up on a white eraser board. Mitch knew it already, but to see the numbers just hovering there in naked defiance of his wishful thinking was galling. The Smith family made more than 98% of all American families, but spent every penny, every month.

Reality Bites

Bill said that the next part of the discussion was to review assets and retirement expectations. Well, that was easy. The Smiths had $500,000 stashed in a few 401(k) accounts, mostly invested in plain vanilla stock index funds. They had about $500,000 in equity in their $2,000,000 house. They had maybe $50,000 in equity in their ski cabin.

Mitchell told Bill that he felt fit and energized enough to keep working until his mid 60s; Gracie could do the same. But they had to admit that they just didn't know how long they would be invited to stay at the corporate party.

After thirty years in sales, Mitch knew how to gauge the energy in a room. He could tell that both he and his wife were feeling comfortable with their advisor Bill. Bill was clearly listening to what they were saying, and had broken the ice enough to earn their trust. Perhaps this is why Bill felt comfortable dropping this bomb:

"Guys, based on what we are discussing here, I am professionally obligated to warn you that your retirement is in great jeopardy. I know $500,000 sounds like a lot, but you're not even close to being able to replace your current income with that. And if, God forbid, someone were to get laid off tomorrow, through no fault of your own, you would run through that $500,000 very quickly."

The words hung weighted in the air. Gracie looked like someone had just slapped her in the face.

"How...how could that be?" she muttered. "Half a million dollars. Half a million! My parents never had that much in their dreams."

Bill remained cool as cucumber. Apparently, this was not his first rodeo. He calmly went over the math.

If they assumed that they both could work until age 67, a *big* "if", then they would earn social security income of about $50,000 combined. By that time, *with good luck*, their $500,000 in the 401(k) would have grown to $800,000. That $800,000 would throw off around $40,000 in passive income if traditional methods were used. So, if they both could make it in the corporate world to 67, then they would still only have around $90,000 in retirement income. They were currently spending $220,000 per year.

Yes, they were looking at a big reduction in expenses because they're youngest daughter was finally finishing college. But even if they saved every penny of that $40,000 for the next 8 years, it just couldn't add up. The Smith family had some tough decisions to make.

They drove home in their shiny Porsche in a state of shock. No one said a word, until they did. Mitch spoke first. "Goddammit, enough with Samantha, enough! Didn't we pay for the best school? Didn't we kill ourselves for her? What are we, a bank?"

"Well, she has to live somewhere safe, Mitch. I'm not going to have my daughter living in a shack. I'm not! And what about this stupid Porsche, who's idea was this?" retorted Gracie.

The fight went from there. An eruption of bitterness, resentment and fear that had been bubbling just under the surface for years. That night, the Smith house got a workout; it seemed like the pair argued in every one of their six bedrooms. Who's fault was this situation? What did they do wrong? What should they do now? Obviously, there had to be big cuts, but it felt like asking the patient to choose which limb she would want amputated first. After a few days of nastiness, what they did was: nothing.

Samantha showed up with her partner Yor, and like clockwork, Gracie wrote her daughter a check. As a balmy Charlotte spring became a scorching southern summer, the air conditioning went out in the house, and Mitch had to pay $5,000 to replace it. It would cost thousands of dollars to break the lease on his Porsche, so he continued to enjoy it with the added pleasure of defiance. Turns out, ignoring problems was easier than Mitch ever would have imagined.

The Winds of Change

They kept it up this way for a number of months. They barely even mentioned that meeting with the financial advisor, and summer was filled with lavish pool parties and vacations. Then Gracie ran into Raquel one day at Whole Foods.

Halfway through customary greetings and salutations, Raquel burst out in tears. She tried to cover her face, but soon her loud sobbing in the produce section was enough to draw attention from the organic, cruelty-free kale and directly to the two women. Gracie had to drag Raquel into the bathroom for some privacy.

Everything was going wrong. Six months had gone by and Barney couldn't find a new job. He had gotten one or two offers from friends to work as a rep, but the pay would be much less than what he was earning before. Raquel continued to work as a pharma rep, but her income just wasn't enough to make ends meet. They hadn't made their mortgage payment last month; they had no idea how they were going to pay their daughter's fall tuition, and now, she had even heard rumors of layoffs at her own company.

It tore Gracie up to see her old gal pal in such a state. Her hair and makeup, typically immaculate for the last several decades, now looked like she had been sprayed by a fire hose. And, other than platitudes, what could Gracie really say? She did her very best to offer compassionate words, but in reality, she wasn't thinking about the Smead family at all. In fact, except for her body, she was barely in that Whole Foods bathroom at all. Her mind was in that office with Bill Anderson and her husband. This was it. No more denial. No more faking it. She wasn't going to let the Smiths wind up like the Smeads. Mitch and Gracie Smith were back in Bill's office within a week. This time, they weren't walking out of there without a plan.

Bill suggested that they break the conversation down into three parts. First, they had to determine which expenses would be cut, and how they would be cut. Second, they had to determine what cash flow that would free up. Lastly, they had to decide how that cash flow would be invested, and what results could be hoped for.

The couple already knew that the big house on the golf course had to go. They could agree on two things: one was that it made no sense for an aging pair of empty nesters to continue living in a six bedroom behemoth, and two was that it would really hurt to sell their dream home. This was the sacred space where they had raised their children and hosted countless warm and cheery barbeques and Christmases. But at a cost of $100,000 a year, the house was undeniably the largest expense that drained them every month.

The next thing that had to go was the Porsche. That stung. There was just no joy in tooling around town in a Hyundai SUV. But it was impossible for Mitchell to ask Gracie to give up the house where she had raised her children without him also giving up his "baby."

The most controversial issue was Samantha. Gracie could not be moved off the idea that her daughter would be in danger if she didn't receive regular financial support. Mitchell loved his daughter dearly, and more than a little part of him wished she was still that playful seven year old running all over their big, sunlit house. But she wasn't seven, rather she was turning twenty-seven and now she seemed to be running wild with money that was needed elsewhere. The couple agreed on the following compromise. Monthly support would be cut from $1,000 to $500, and that $500 would be on a credit card that the elder Smiths controlled. Mitch and Gracie wanted to see exactly where that money was going. It had certainly occurred to Mitch that his ever more tattooed daughter could have a drug problem. At least with this compromise he wouldn't be fueling any bad habits.

Establishing and committing to a concrete cost-cutting plan made Mitchell nauseous. At times he felt like his head was swimming and he had to grip onto the arms of his chair to keep himself from floating away. However, the next part made him happier. Much happier.

They would keep the ski cabin, and continue to build equity in it with an eye on living there in retirement. By selling the main house, they could achieve two main goals. First, they would be freeing up an extra $500,000 in capital that could be invested to create retirement income. Second, they would be cutting their monthly housing expense from $9000 to just $3500 (They aimed to move into a luxurious two bedroom rental in a similar golf community to where they were currently living). When combined with the savings achieved by returning the Porsche and cutting back on Samantha, they could now look forward to saving $7000 per month, or about $84,000 a year.

Because the couple enjoyed fabulous 401(k) matches from their work, Bill suggested that about half of that money go directly from their paycheck into their 401(k). This way they could count on a generous company matching contribution, and reduce the temptation to spend the money. A juicy $42,000 would never pass through their hands; rather, it would go straight to retirement.

With the company match, the Smiths could plan on socking away as much as $62,000 per year into their 401(k). Bill suggested that the couple select a high dividend exchange traded fund for that money. They chose to divide the money between the Spdr S&P Global Dividend ETF (Ticker: WDIV) and the iShares Core High Dividend ETF (Ticker: HDV). That way, the dividends would compound tax free over the next nine years, and the couple would be able to build confidence in their passive income stream. They would be able to check their quarterly statements four times a year and watch the dividends come in. This should help with that queasy feeling every time there was a rumor of layoffs.

For the other $42,000, Bill suggested a diversified portfolio of closed-end funds. (Reviewed in Chapter 12 of this book). The plain truth was that they were currently so far behind in their retirement savings that the simple 2% dividend yield of typical stocks wasn't going to do it. Bill illustrated how the couple could hope to generate 6% monthly income, tax preferred, by investing in a range of CEFs. Ultimately, they chose a suite of established CEFs like Cohen & Steers Infrastructure Fund (Ticker: UTF), Doubleline Income Solutions (Ticker: DSL), The Black Rock Enhanced Global Dividend Trust (Ticker: BOE), and the Pimco High Income Fund (Ticker: PHK).

Lastly, there was the matter of the $500,000 that would become available after the sale of the house. For this pot of money, Bill suggested a "high low" strategy. Since the couple had been in the medical business their whole lives, they felt very comfortable investing half in constant dividend growers such as

Big Pharma and medical device stocks. They would expect a quarterly dividend in the 3% range with these stocks, and that payout would likely grow dramatically as they aged. For the other half of the money, they could purchase mortgage REITs. Although these were more *high beta* (high volatility) than their other investments, they would need the high income. A monthly 9% paycheck would help to cushion the blow in case they couldn't work until age 67.

For the Big Pharma portion of the portfolio, Bill and the Smiths chose names that they knew and trusted: Pfizer (Ticker: PFE), Eli Lilly (Ticker: LLY), Bristol Myers Squibb (Ticker: BMS), Abbot (Ticker: ABT), Medtronic (Ticker: MDT) and Stryker (Ticker: SYK). You may remember that we discussed Big Pharma stocks in Chapter 6.

For the mortgage REIT half of this portfolio, Bill steered them to three of the biggest names in the business, Annaly Capital Management (Ticker: NLY), AGNC Investment Corp (Ticker: AGNC), and Blackstone Mortgage Trust (Ticker: BXMT).

Bill ran the following simulation. If they continued to grow their current 401(k) savings at a steady rate of 8% and could grow the $500,000 from their house at a rate of 7%, then they could have almost $1,800,000 by the time Mitchell turned 67 and could collect social security.

But the big reductions in lifestyle really made the difference. If the couple saved $135,000 a year over the next nine years (the money saved from lifestyle cuts, plus their second daughter finishing college, plus 401(k) match), and they earned an average return of 8%, then they could expect to add $1,686,000. If everything went to plan, Mitch and Gracie could be looking at a 3,800,000 nest egg by age 67.

If their investments threw off 6% in yearly income, they could look forward to a tax preferred income of $228,000 plus around $50,000 in social security. That would easily pay for their more modest lifestyle and still enable them to put some gold in their golden years.

Bill was careful to caution that those projections were only if everything went just right. The Smiths absolutely had to follow through on their lifestyle cuts. They both needed to put in every possible effort to remain employed until age 67. And of course, they needed some luck in the market. Bill chose a projected return of 8%, lower than the market's average return, to take into account taxes and the ups and downs of the market. But in reality, they could experience a market crash during the following nine years. No one has a crystal ball. Luckily, by dramatically cutting their expenses and ramping up saving, their retirement would likely survive all but the most dire scenarios.

What an emotional rollercoaster ride had just occurred in Bill Anderson's office. The dejection and disgust at having to sell the house, the fear when going through the numerical scenarios, and the sheer elation when Bill announced that, not only could the couple's retirement be salvaged, but could actually look quite rosey!

After decades of success in the cut throat world of corporate sales, the Smith family knew what it meant to strive towards a goal. They had thrived under pressure for many years, and rarely failed to meet quota. This challenge would be no different. They left that office with a strong feeling of purpose; they knew what they needed to do. As Mitch and Gracie jumped in the Porsche for the last time, they put down the top and enjoyed an exhilarating ride. Somehow it just seemed so much more fun to drive when you finally knew where you were going.

TABLE 3: The Smith Family Finances (All numbers are Annualized)

His Income	$230,000	
Her Income	$110,000	
Total Pre Tax	$340,000	
Total Take Home Pay	$220,000	
	Old Expenses	New Expenses
House	$100,000	$42,000
Food & Entertainment	$20,000	$20,000
Porsche	$12,000	$0
Mountain Cabin	$30,000	$30,000
College Expense	$40,000	$0
Educational Loan	$7,000	$7,000
Daughter Support	$12,000	$6,000
Total Expenses	$221,000	$105,000
Available to Invest	$0	$115,000
401 K Match	$0	$20,000
Total To Invest, yearly	$0	$135,000

Growth of Smith Assets, New plan vrs Old Plan

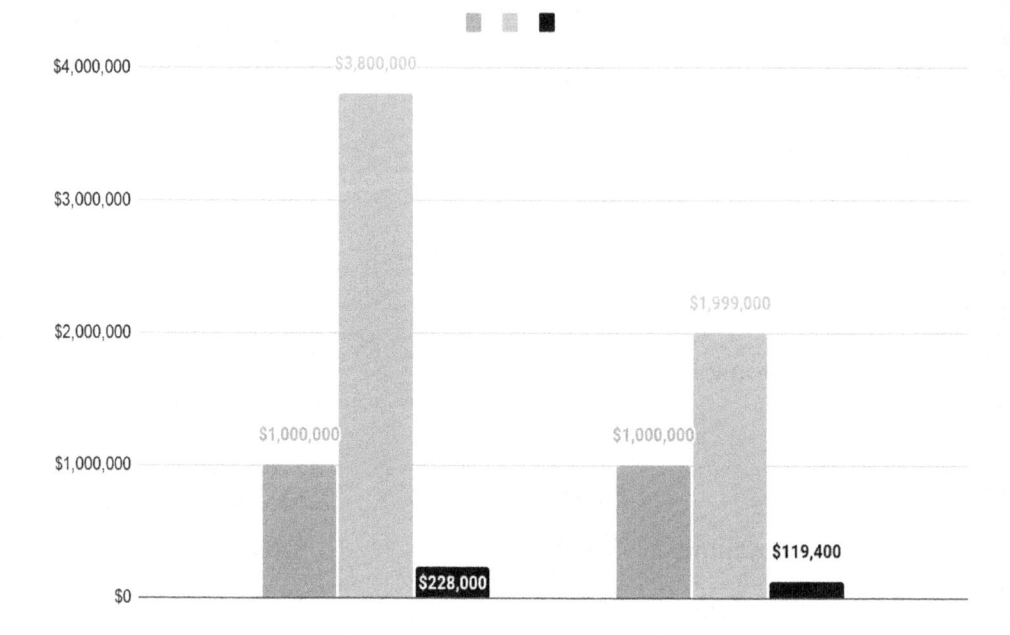

$4,000,000	$3,800,000
$3,000,000	
$2,000,000	$1,999,000
$1,000,000	$1,000,000 $1,000,000
	$228,000 $119,400
$0	

Figure 8

The far left column is the family's current assets. The middle column assumes the assets grow at 8% rate over the next 9 years. (Remember that the new Smith Family Plan includes $135,000 a year in extra savings.) The last column on the right represents the annual income the family can expect from their assets at age 67.

Suggested Assets for New Smith Retirement Plan

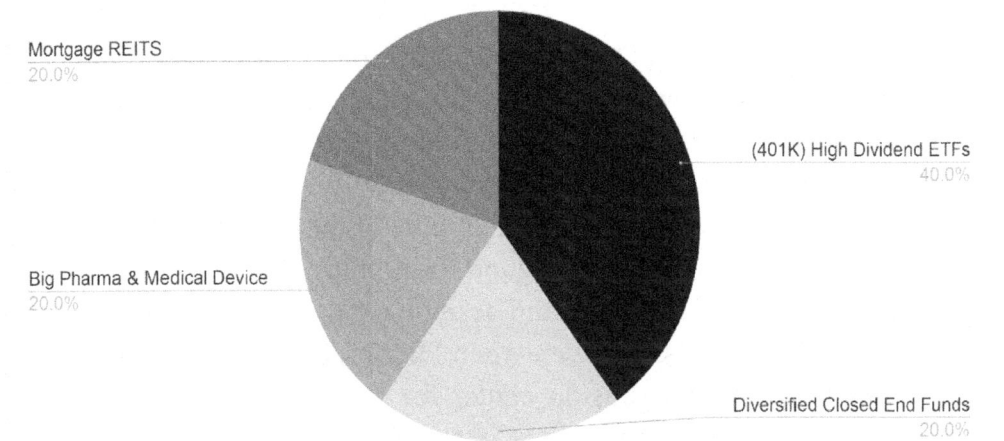

Mortgage REITS
20.0%

(401K) High Dividend ETFs
40.0%

Big Pharma & Medical Device
20.0%

Diversified Closed End Funds
20.0%

Figure 9

Chapter 17: Model Portfolio - The Retiree "Forever Young"

It just wasn't fair. Dolores struggled with the thought day and night. She knew that only the Lord got to determine matters of life and death, but the bitterness still felt like a leaden weight she carried around with her all day. When her ever more frail husband needed help in the middle of the night to crawl to the toilet. When her lousy, good-for-nothing daughter looked right past her dying father and asked how much money would be left when he passed. Even when Dolores escorted her failing husband to the transfusion center for his chemotherapy, she wanted to scream at the doctor, at the nurses, at the world, "It's not fair!"

Her husband Gonzalo had done nothing but care for this family since age 19 when he and Dolores had left everything and everyone they had ever known in Nicaragua and came to America on a wing and a prayer. He was 19 and she was 17; they spoke no English. Soon, Gonzalo wasn't even old enough to order a beer in his new country and he had one baby and another on the way.

She tried to be happy and upbeat, but it was tough. Sometimes when he was sitting in the infusion chair, reading a magazine in the cold, sterile light of the clinic, she would stare at the living skeleton who had once been Gonzalo Rodriguez. Was this really the young man who had come to America at 19 and worked tirelessly, six days a week, decade after decade to provide for his three children and his wife? Was this the same man who displayed endless patience when his eldest daughter showed up at their house, constantly pregnant with no partner to speak of? This was supposed to be *their* time together. Their golden years.

Finally, Gonzalo had paid off the house, finally there were no more children or grandchildren living with them. Finally, she convinced Gonzalo to hand off the air conditioning business to their son and retire at age 72. They were supposed to travel, to go out to dinner with friends, to finally live a little before dying. And now this. Cancer. Not fair.

It was also more than a little upsetting to hear that people just seemed to want to talk about money. With doctors trying treatment after treatment, sometimes with limited success, sometimes not, and Gonzalo looking worse by the week, people wanted to know how they were going to be living when Papa was gone. Her son wanted Gonzalo to sign some paperwork so that he officially owned the AC business. It wasn't much, just a few guys and a truck, but that little AC business had helped the Rodriguez family make a life in a strange new land. Her good-for-nothing daughter just wanted to grub for whatever handout she could get; no surprise there. Only her youngest daughter, Jennifer, seemed genuinely concerned about Dolores. Jennifer had been on her own since age 18. Gonzalo and Dolores had given her what they could to afford college, but mostly she made her own way with a combination of loans and scholarships. Today, she was a married mother of two and had some kind of job in finance. No matter how many times Jennifer had tried to explain the job, Dolores didn't really understand what her *hija* did every day. Oh well. When she drove to Jennifer's house, which would have looked like some kind of dream palace to her cousins back in Nicaragua, with her all American kids playing football in the yard and her gringo husband grilling something up by the sparkling suburban pool, it was just pure joy for Dolores. "All worth it," she thought to herself. At least here she and Gonzalo had done something right.

She assumed that her daughter could afford the nice suburban house. Just like her daughter assumed the elder Rodriguezes could afford to retire. Dolores assumed that whatever amount of money they had, it was enough. The bills were always paid. She knew Gonzalo had finally paid off the mortgage. But other than that, no one ever really talked about money. Not that it was some kind of big secret, but it just felt like a private subject. Asking Jennifer about money would have felt like asking about her sex life. Just sort of weird and icky.

Dolores had always been the family caregiver. She was pregnant for the first time by age 17; caring for three rambunctious children in her mid-20s was no easy feat. Caring for three rebellious teens in her 30s wasn't much easier. In her 40s, when life was supposed to get easier, her own elderly mother arrived from Nicaragua to live in their house, and the middle daughter seemed to show up every few years with a new baby that she didn't really feel like caring for. Between caring for her own demented mother in her 40s and 50s, and trying to raise unwanted grandchildren for her constantly troubled middle daughter, the time just went by. Gonzalo went to work, they lived simply, bills got paid. Money wasn't really her department.

When he was initially diagnosed, Gonzalo remained upbeat and vigorous. But with each passing month, and each failed chemo treatment, the life seemed to leak out of him bit by bit. Soon he told her he was satisfied with his time here on Earth, and ready to come face to face with the Lord when he was called home. This seemed to comfort Gonzalo, but Dolores was inconsolable. She had met him in her village in Nicaragua when she was 16. Could there even be a life without him?

Gonzalo was the one who called Jennifer for a private family meeting. The other two Rodriguez children were not invited. "I've got bad news, and I've got good news," was the first thing he said.

The bad news was that the doctor had told him to get his affairs in order. The other bad news was that the last three years of cancer therapy had been very expensive. Even though they had Medicare, there were still a lot of big expenses that Medicare didn't cover, and he had been forced to spend most of the couple's retirement savings.

The good news, he said, was that "he was worth more dead than alive." Years ago, he had purchased life insurance that would take care of Dolores in her old age. He tried to laugh as he said it, but it just came out as a wheezing cough. Dolores didn't think any of it was "good" news. She ran out of the room crying and didn't hear any more of the details. She didn't care about any details. She would have given every last penny to keep Gonzalo alive. But it wasn't to be.

A Life for Dolores

The rest went by in a flash. Years later, she could just remember bits and pieces. The stench of bleach in the hospital, the flickering lights in the church, phone calls from cousins she hadn't spoken to in years. The first few awful nights of being in her house alone. In fifty years, she couldn't remember spending a night alone in that *casa*. Now it was her new reality.

Soon, a new feeling crept in. Something that had never even occurred to her during Gonzalo's long, slow decline. Fear. Sure, she had money coming to her. But what if she screwed up? She barely knew how to write a check. She had very rarely looked at the charges on their credit card. She would get one big payout, just one big chance. What if she screwed up and lost everything? Would she wind up the old crazy *abuela* living in Jennifer's house? Or worse?

Just a few weeks after the funeral, the check came in the mail. So strange. Just a simple piece of mail; on the outside no different than a bank statement, or an ad from a mortgage company. Except this one held a check for $500,000 with her name on it. When she took the check out of the envelope, she must have stared at it for half an hour. Her hands were trembling when she deposited the check at her local bank.

Soon, she had another sit down with Jennifer, and her youngest daughter went over the current situation with her.

Dolores owned her house outright. It was no mansion, but it was a well kept, clean home in a nice, safe neighborhood. Jennifer, who by her late 40s had already owned several homes, estimated that the maintenance and taxes on the house would be about $1,000 a month.

Dolores also owned her own car, free and clear. Sure, it was a ten-year-old Honda, but it worked. Since Dolores actually drove very little, the car had low mileage on it. Even so, an old car was an old car, and it could need some maintenance. Jennifer figured that cost at $5,000 per year.

If there was one thing that Dolores had learned to do while raising three kids, several grandkids, and taking care of friends and neighbors, it was cook. Everyone wanted a taste of her famous *pupusas* and other Nicaraguan dishes. It was tasty, but not expensive. So Jennifer estimated Dolores's food costs at about $4,000 per year.

At age 70, Dolores was in pretty good shape. Other than the standard pills for cholesterol and blood pressure, she had really only been in the hospital as a visitor. Still, the whole ordeal with Gonzalo had taught the Rodriguez family that old age could be expensive. So Jennifer estimated $4,000 per year in medical costs.

All of this added up meant that Dolores needed about $25,000 a year just to keep the lights on. In other words, since she already owned a home and car, $25,000 would be enough for her to maintain basic independence, although she would have almost no money left over for hobbies or fun. As a surviving spouse, she could count on $25,000 a year in social security money, guaranteed from the government (although some of that would be taxed, leading to less spendable income). So how should she invest the $500,000 in life insurance money to meet her needs?

Jennifer presented three different options. Dolores could earn about 3% annually by depositing her money in very safe, very secure, traditional options like municipal bonds, long term treasuries, and a few blue chip stocks. This would yield $15,000 annually. All of Dolores's basic bills would be paid, but she had better adopt some cheap hobbies, and forget giving anything to her church or her grandchildren. Also, if she were unlucky enough to live into really old age, and inflation ever surpassed 3% annually, she could suffer a dotage of real poverty.

The next option was to invest somewhat more aggressively, aiming for a 5% annual return. This would provide Dolores with roughly $25,000 in annual income. This would be a mix of traditional, ultra safe investments like municipal bonds, and a few higher dividend paying stocks and REITs. This portfolio could see its total value fluctuate more than the ultra conservative portfolio, but it would mean that Dolores could take one trip per year, and eat out once or twice a week.

The last option was a more aggressive portfolio aiming to yield about 7% annually. This would give Dolores $35,0000 a year in passive income, for a total pre-tax income of $60,0000. Since she already owned her house and car, this would mean that Dolores would have as much as $19,0000 a year to travel, go to dinner with friends, and even spoil her grandchildren. The 7% portfolio would consist mostly of closed end funds, preferred shares, and REITs. While the principal balance could fluctuate significantly, the income would be robust and reliable.

It all made Dolores's head hurt. There was a lot to think about. A lot of different considerations. When she asked Jennifer which option she thought was best, Jennifer simply replied, "They're all just fine choices. I guess it really depends on how active you want to be, and how much up and down you can stand with your money." Dolores took a month to think it all over.

Dolores's Choice

It was a lot to consider. But she felt less scared with Jennifer lending support. She also had the strangest feeling; it was like Gonzalo had never died at all, like he was right there with her to help her decide. Of course, he wasn't there to speak physically, but it was his money too; his hard work to take care of his family, even in the afterlife. She pretty much knew what he would say.

When speaking of their eldest daughter, she of the random children, she of the brushes with the law, she of the "occasional mother" act, Dolores knew that Gonzalo had finally just had enough. They had practically raised two of her four children, and who even knew where the other two were now? In fact, the grandchildren themselves were just arriving at the age where they could conceivably show up on Dolores' doorstep with a little bundle of joy, expecting that *abuela's* now empty house could be a daycare center, or an orphanage altogether. She could picture her late husband turning purple with rage, but struggling not to speak ill of his own kin; "It's not for us to judge, it's for the Lord to judge, but Lord help her, because I've just had enough of this *mierda!*" He would say. If Dolores stuck around the house too much due to low income, then that no-good daughter of hers might see she had nothing to do, and *find* something for her to do.

Her middle child, her son, had his father's business now. He seemed content enough. So, the first child deserved no inheritance, and the second child had already got an inheritance. Anything left over when Dolores went to reunite with Gonzalo could go to Jennifer, although she really didn't need it. All of which meant that Dolores only needed enough money to live out the rest of her life.

Once again, she could feel Gonzalo advising her from heaven, "So live! Live while you are still living, *mi querida!* Take those trips!" Before the diagnosis, they had both been excited about the prospect of traveling the world in retirement. Truthfully, it had been her idea. She knew that her church ran all kinds of trips to special places, like the Vatican and Israel, and even special pilgrimage sites around Europe. He had wanted to go on these trips, but he just couldn't see himself not having to work anymore. After fifty years of labor with his hands, the splendor of the Vatican just didn't seem like it could be for the Rodriguez family. But now it was. The money was there. Jennifer had done the math twice. With Gonzalo, or with Gonzalo in spirit, Dolores Rodriguez could realistically set foot in the Holy Land. Imagine that! A trip to Israel. The poor girl from a Nicaraguan village living long enough to see the very spot where her Lord and Savior had walked the Earth and preached his Gospel. She felt something growing inside of her that she hadn't felt in years. Joy. Joy!

So, clearly, the idea of seeing the world in her old age was exciting to her. But what were the risks? Well, Jennifer had warned her that the higher yielding portfolio could fluctuate up and down in value. Maybe she could even lose some money. But she owned her house, free and clear. That wouldn't fluctuate much. Her Social Security check was as much of a sure thing as there is in this life. At some point, keeping the house would be impossible anyhow. As a fit, youngish retiree she could continue to maintain a single family home. But she would probably have to sell it in her 80s anyhow, if she actually made it that far. And by that time, her major traveling days would probably be done, so how much money would she really need, anyhow? At any rate, Jennifer emphasized that the 7% portfolio would very likely throw off great income for years to come; it was just a little more volatile than the other options. Something could go wrong, but probably not. Dolores has survived coming to a new country with no language skills and little education, and somehow raised three kids in her new country. She could probably survive a few ups and downs in the stock market in exchange for the ability to finally have some "me time" at the end of her life. 7% it was.

Jennifer and Dolores began a process of exploration, and after a couple of months of deliberation, chose the following investments.

They chose Iron Mountain (Ticker: IRM), Kinder Morgan (Ticker: KMI), and Lumen Technologies (Ticker, LUMN) as three fallen angel stocks. (We learned about this technique in Chapter 3).

They chose the exchange traded fund iShares Preferred and Income Securities (Ticker: PFF) as their core investment in preferred shares. They also chose some preferred shares from Bank of America, NextEra Energy, and AmTrust Financial Services. (See Chapter 11 to review preferred shares).

In the closed-end fund sector, they chose to focus on utility funds and municipal bond funds. Jennifer felt that these were the safest sectors. They bought Reaves Utility Income (Ticker: UTG), BlackRock Muniyield Quality Fund II (Ticker: MQT), and the Gabelli Utility Trust (Ticker: GUT). (Check Chapter 12 to review CEFs).

Finally, they sprinkled in some REITs and mortgage REITs, purchasing Sabra Healthcare REIT (Ticker: SBRA), W.P. Carey (Ticker: WPC), and Annaly Capital Management (Ticker: NLY).

Soon, all of the investment arrangements were made. In no time, investment income started showing up in her brokerage account like clockwork. Dolores went out to dinner with friends. She made a donation to a charity. She bought some nice Christmas gifts for her grandchildren.

Finally, the day came when she felt comfortable booking that church trip to Israel. She blinked back tears when the salesperson asked her how many tickets she needed to buy. "Just one," she said. Even though he wouldn't be needing a ticket, she knew Gonzalo would be with her.

TABLE 4: Dolores Rodriguez's Finances

PreTax Income	$60,000
Post Tax	$48,000
Home Maintenance & Taxes	$12,000
Car Maintenance	$5,000
Food	$4,000
Medical	$4,000
Grandkids & Miscellaneous	$4,000
Travel & Entertainment	$19,000

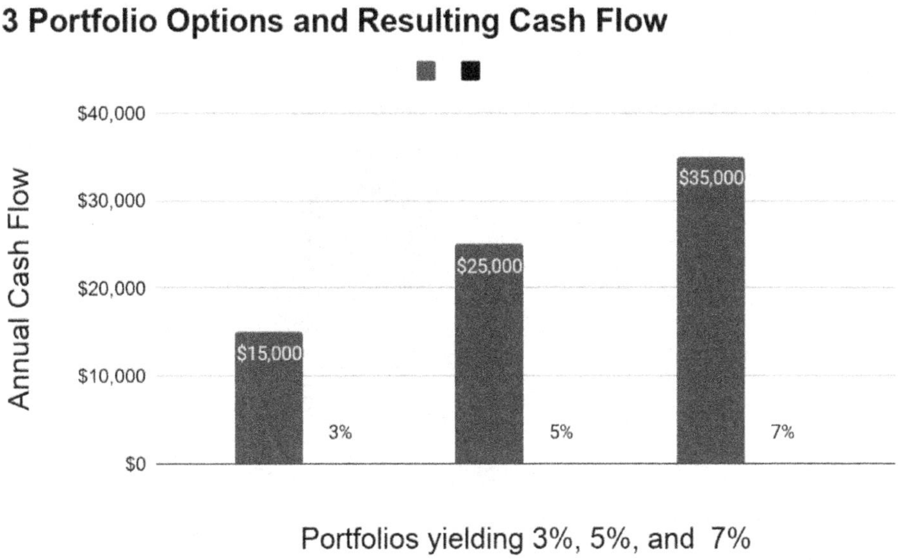
3 Portfolio Options and Resulting Cash Flow
Annual Cash Flow
$40,000
$30,000
$20,000
$10,000
$0
$15,000
$25,000
$35,000
3%
5%
7%
Portfolios yielding 3%, 5%, and 7%

Figure 10

This illustration assumes that Dolores is investing $500,000. These cash flows do not factor in her social security income.

Suggested Investments for Dolores (7% Portfolio)

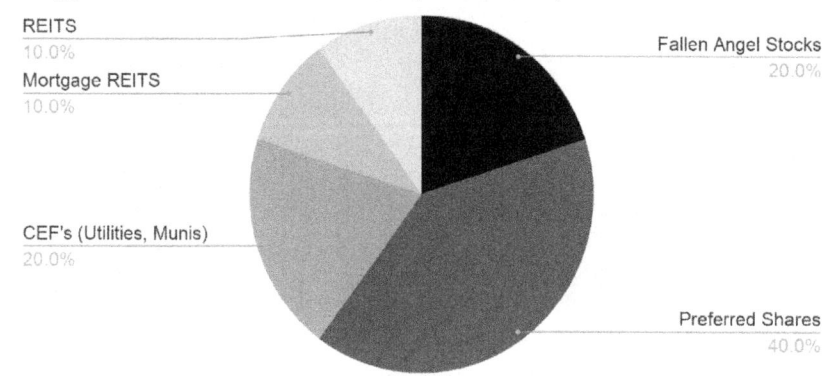

- REITS 10.0%
- Mortgage REITS 10.0%
- CEF's (Utilities, Munis) 20.0%
- Fallen Angel Stocks 20.0%
- Preferred Shares 40.0%

Figure 11

Chapter 18: The Knowledge Dividend

"An investment in knowledge pays the best interest."
-Benjamin Franklin

With this chapter, we come to the end of our book. My fervent hope is that the end of this book is only the beginning of your journey into knowledge.

In today's world, you can't avoid constant discussion about the growing gap between the "haves" and the "have nots." Let me tell you, if you have the intelligence, drive, and determination to have finished this book, you already have a whole lot more than a lot of people. There is no reason in the world why you can't position yourself firmly in the "have" column of our rapidly bifurcating society.

To have money, it really helps to have knowledge first. Even though knowledge is more valuable than ever, amazingly, you can access most of the knowledge you need for cheap or even free. The information that you can get for free on your E-Trade account with the stroke of a few keys used to take numerous trips to the library for your parents or grandparents. You can do a lot of the same reading that a Harvard MBA would do for the simple price of a subscription to the Wall Street Journal or Barron's magazine. In that spirit, please find a list of recommended resources at the end of this chapter. Many are free.

As I write this, I am sitting in a park, sipping a cup of coffee. Today, I woke up when I felt like it. After I finish this chapter, I may go have a beer in the middle of the day to celebrate the successful completion of another book. One beer on a hot afternoon is a terrific celebration of my freedom.

I say this not to arouse jealousy or to boast. I say this because I am not any better than you. I don't have any special formal education (I have an undergraduate history degree). I am not smarter or even luckier than anyone else (I suffered plenty of painful failures along the way). I just had a burning desire to release myself from the corporate chains that bound me. If you have selected, purchased, and read this book, you probably have a similar desire. If I made it happen through passive income investing, then you can too.

The Takeaway

When I think of business books that I have read in the past, what seems to separate the excellent books from standard books is that the excellent books made just a few key, memorable points. I can tell you a few books that I read decades ago where a few key points still stand out in my mind.

Have I written an excellent book? I don't know; I hope so. But here are three key points that you should take with you long after this book starts gathering dust in your library:

1. Rich people don't work hard. Rich people have everyone else working hard for them. This is not a nice statement. This is not a fair statement. But it reflects reality. The reason why I can sit here in the park and write this text today is because I know that, on the first of the month, I have payment coming to me from the companies that I own. Those companies employ thousands of people who work hard every day so that I don't have to.

And I am still an amateur! Just this week, I read a headline that Bill Gates got a quarterly dividend check from Microsoft for $57,000,000. He hasn't worked there in at least a decade. Walmart, one of the largest companies in the world, is still controlled by the Walton family. They haven't shown up to do a day of work at their own company in multiple decades.

When faced with this reality, we can sit around and complain about how unfair it is, or we can figure out what these people all have in common, and try to emulate their ways. What the Waltons and Gates and even myself all have in common is: ownership. We own companies. The Waltons own 50% of Walmart, while I own 0.00005%. But the general principles are the same. Use the tactics and techniques in this book to put yourself in the same position.

2. Don't be afraid to shop for equity securities that pay higher dividends than average. As we reviewed in this book, many of the largest companies that you are familiar with are obscene money machines. They churn out indecent cash flows year after year, decade after decade. They only pay 1 or 2% dividends because they feel like it. They could easily pay higher dividends, but for a variety of reasons that we covered in chapter 2, they prefer to use the cash in other ways. Stocks that pay double or even triple the norm are not necessarily suspicious or suspect. They simply choose to pay out their cash instead of buyback stock or buy other companies. The simple difference between a portfolio that yields 2% and a portfolio that yields 6% can be life changing.

3. You may have noticed from our case studies that, surprisingly, the highest income people did not always have the easiest path to retirement. To use the old adage, "It ain't what you make, it's what you keep." This book is chock full of methods of maximizing income from your savings, but if you don't have

much savings, you will have a very hard time generating passive income, no matter how much you make from your job.

Trust me when I tell you that I have known people who earn millions, *millions,* but also somehow spend millions. They wind up just as stressed out and depressed as someone working at Target and living in a trailer park. "It ain't what you make, it's what you keep." In just a page or two, you will find a list of cheap or free resources that will provide you all the knowledge you will ever need to turn your savings into a passive income machine. But only you know how to monitor or control your own spending. Too much spending means too little savings, and that means little freedom in your life.

I'll close with one last saying: "Freedom ain't free." Sadly, it ain't. Even though in America we are all born free on paper, every day millions of people spend their precious time on this Earth doing things they don't want to do because they are locked in the invisible cage of poverty. Very often, they are not just poor in money; they are also poor in knowledge. Your newfound financial knowledge is the key that will set you free.

When will your day of liberation come? It may not be tomorrow, or even the next day. But if you use the principals you have learned in this book, trust me, it's just a matter of time until you break free. Financial freedom, viewed by millions of people as an impossibility, will become your inevitable reality.

Suggested Reading Resources

Kiplinger's Magazine (Cheap)
Wall Street Journal (Cheap)
Barron's Magazine (Cheap)

Seeking Alpha (Free/cheap, depending on membership)
Investopedia.com (Free)
Dividend.com (Free)
CEF Connect (cefconnect.com) (Free)
SureDividend.com (cheap)
DividendDetective.com (Free/cheap)
Reit.com (Free)
Reitnotes.com (Free/cheap)
The High Yield Landlord Newsletter (Leonberg Capital) (Cheap)

Accounting for Dummies (Free/cheap)
Reading Financial Reports for Dummies (Free/cheap)
The Millionaire Next Store, Thomas J. Stanley, PhD (Free/cheap)
Rich Dad, Poor Dad, Robert Kiyosaki (Free/cheap)
Fed Up: An Insider's Take on why the Federal Reserve is Bad for America, Danielle DiMartino Booth (Free/cheap)

Made in the USA
Columbia, SC
23 December 2023